The Portland Career Hunter's Guide

"But I don't even know what I want to do!"
Turn to Chapter 2.

"I'm ready to start a career search, but I don't know how to begin."
Turn to Chapter 3.

"I know what I'm good at, but I don't know what kind of job uses those skills."
Turn to Chapter 2.

"I don't think my resume is very good."
Turn to Chapter 3.

"I'm scared stiff in a job interview."
Turn to Chapter 3.

"Where do I get the right names and addresses of people in my new field?"
Turn to Chapter 5.

"I'm afraid I'll take a job and find I don't fit in with the people there!"
Turn to Chapters 2 and 5.

"You mean I can get the name of the Marketing Director for the San Francisco office?"
Turn to Chapter 5.

"But who wants to hire someone with a BA in Psychology?"
Turn to Chapter 2.

"What should I do after I've had an interview and want to show them I really want that job?"

Turn to Chapter 3.

"What happens if I really screw up in an interview and want another chance to talk with people at the company?"

Turn to Chapter 3.

"What's the use of having a resume? They just get thrown in a pile with all the rest!"

Turn to Chapter 3.

"How do I know if an agency can help me solve my career-hunting problems?"

Turn to Chapter 1.

"I'm getting depressed. I've been job-hunting for months now, with no luck."

Turn to Chapters 1, 2, 3, 4, 5, and 6.

"I must be doing something wrong. I know I'm qualified for jobs, but I never get called back for a second interview!"

Turn to Chapter 3.

"How do I know what kinds of careers will be useful in ten years?"

Turn to Chapter 5.

"How do I explain holes in my background or unfavorable events? I got fired from my last job!"

Turn to Chapter 3.

Portland Career Hunter's Guide

A Sourcebook of Local Resources
for the Serious Career Planner
and Job-Hunter

by SHERI RADERS

Victoria House — Portland, Oregon

I would like to extend a sincere thank you to everyone who helped me with this project. Without the support and persistence of those friends, I may never have maintained the self-discipline to finish it.

ISBN 0-918480-04-3
Library of Congress Card Catalog Number: 77-20519

Photo credit: Reid Neubert.

For my family in Iowa:
Helen, Lou and Jim

TABLE OF CONTENTS

1. Starting Out: A Look at Strategy

Some thoughts to help you:

choose your job-finding method

figure out where you need help

learn where to find that help

understand the limits of these resources

possess a basic knowledge of
the Portland-area economy

Most of us who have thought at all about our career options have a persistent fantasy: A benevolent employer will come calling on us one day with the **perfect** job opportunity. Or we will be pleasantly napping one afternoon and the phone will ring: "Hello...We have a job here for you whenever you are ready...." That happens... but not very often. Most of the time, you have to create the opportunity.

As a job-hunter you are repeatedly told that the task of

changing careers or finding a job is itself a full-time job, that you should strap yourself to the task and work at it until you have suited your career needs. Eight hours a day if possible — at least five days a week.

It **is** a demanding job; it **does** take a great deal of time. But most of us find it difficult to persist, or we do not know exactly what we are supposed to be doing with those eight hours. The self-help books on job-hunting are tremendously useful — but they cannot make that job magically appear. The cold hard fact is this: You must do it yourself. No one will bring you a job on a silver platter. However, there **are** people and agencies who can help you. And their numbers are growing. The increasing awareness of the important role our jobs play in our lives has given birth to an entire field of vocational services.

This is a book about the help that is available in Portland to you, the career-seeker. In the Portland area there are many agencies and individuals who can lend advice, direction, and support in your search. They can help you plan those eight hours and teach you to use them efficiently.

Lay Out Your Strategy

I cannot over-emphasize the importance of having a planned job strategy. You need to know **how** you intend to go about the work. Fortunately, there are some fine paperback books available which can help you decide how to do this. Two of the best are Richard Bolles' "What Color Is Your Parachute?" and Richard Irish's "Go Hire Yourself an Employer." These two entertaining books deserve all the acclaim they receive, and they are packed with information you should have before dragging yourself up and down the streets or sending out two hundred resumes in a futile effort.

Then Take Action: Self-Marketing

When you have tentatively selected some kind of job-finding strategy, even a sketchy one, the book you are reading now will serve you well. It is a "where-to" sourcebook rather than a "how-to" job strategy book. It enumerates the places in Portland where you can find help in all phases of the vocational selection process.

Those phases can be easily understood if you look on job-finding as a case of self-marketing.

• **You need to know your product.**

What skills do you possess?

What do you want to do with them?

Where do you want to live?

What kind of people do you like to work with?

What kind of working environment do you need?

Why do you want to change jobs?

- **You need to know your potential market.**

  Who can best use your talents?

  Would you fit in there?

  What are the hiring practices?

  What can they offer you now?

  In the future?

- **You need to know how to communicate your product to your market.**

  Will the conventional channels work?

  Or is there a ''good ole boy'' network operating?

  Who is the person who actually has the power to hire you?

  How have others made successful careers there?

- **You must refine your salesmanship to finalize your sale.**

  Is your resume working for you?

  Do you perform well in job interviews?

  Are you prepared in every conceivable way to meet with people who are in a position to offer you a job?

Resources in Portland

There are agencies in Portland, both public and private, which can help you through each of these career-hunting phases. The help includes counseling and testing services to help you decide what you want to do, as well as workshops and classes to help you learn job-finding skills. There are resume preparation services, placement centers, and employment agencies. There are more sources than you can imagine to provide you with information about careers, working, companies, and industries.

Each agency in this book is described in terms of:
- how it functions
- how it is staffed
- what its services cost
- who is eligible to use them
- how it differs from other agencies performing the same kinds of tasks.

15 •

The description of each agency is presented as objectively as possible; the information speaks for itself in most cases. However, when you are considering using any of them you should remain very clear about one thing: You are employing **them** to do something for **you.** In that light, be sure to find out if their services are right for you. Interview them before you accept their help. Employers interview you before hiring you, so employ that same strategy when selecting someone to help you in your career search. It is certain that some agencies will serve you better or less expensively than others. Make sure that their product meets your particular needs. Make lots of notes. I tried to leave room at the head of the agency listings for you to note date you contacted them, whom you spoke to, follow-up needed, etc. Scribble in the margins if you need to. This book will provide you with information to help you make your decision more easily, but you should still shop around before making a final choice.

The research for this book was undertaken with the goal of serving the needs of career-oriented people — people who view their careers as a way of life as well as a way to live. Therefore, some job-finding agencies in the area have been excluded. For example, programs designed exclusively for young people have been omitted, as have most of the placement agencies for unskilled workers. The agencies and individuals included here are aimed toward people who have focused on careers as more than a means to put bread and wine on the table.

The methodology used to unearth these agencies was anything but sophisticated; I snooped and snooped until I felt I had discovered everything. I used the yellow pages of the phone book, watched the newspapers for information, contacted the educational institutions which offer services to the public, and canvassed the government agencies. And the first thing I learned is that many professionals in the field of vocational counseling and guidance are not aware of the other professionals in the area! There has not been a prior compendium of these services, and it is here that I acknowledge that undoubtedly I may have missed some individuals and agencies which would be appropriately included. If the number is discovered to be significant, the new information can be compiled for a revised edition of this work.

I visited almost all the agencies. In a few cases, such as the resume preparation services, a telephone call was sufficient to learn the facts. However, most of the time I followed a phone call with a personal appointment and spent as much time as possible with an agency representative. I am confident of the accuracy of the information at the time of this writing. However, you should be aware that some of the material changes rapidly, and you might find that an agency head has been replaced or that costs have changed. Again, be sure to investigate an agency for yourself to make sure the information is current before entering into a commitment.

First You Find Out Where to Begin

Chapter 2, "Finding a Suitable Career," describes the services in the Portland area which are designed to help you evaluate your skills and decide what you would like to do with them. Here you find public agencies such as the community colleges, government agencies, and grant programs, as well as a host of private agencies including clinical psychologists and vocational guidance centers. Each is presented with information about costs, time requirements, and the procedures you need to follow to take advantage of the services. The interest and aptitude tests you might encounter are briefly described.

17 •

Chapter 3, "Learning Job-Finding Skills," deals with developing that essential second set of skills you need to actually land the job you want. These job-finding skills are almost as important as your vocational skills. This chapter analyzes the classes, workshops, seminars, and support groups designed to teach you the ins and outs of job-hunting, including resume preparation, interviewing techniques, communication skills, follow-up procedures, and "tricks" of job-hunting. Private resume preparation services are included here as well as adult education classes, government services, and private support services.

Chapter 4, "Immediate Job Access," outlines local sources of job listings. Some of these, such as the employment agencies and state services, are presented here with a method to help you evaluate them for your own purposes. Employment agencies in particular can be valuable if you understand **exactly** what they can and cannot do for you. Government services include the State Employment Service, the civil service boards of the state, county, city, and federal governments, and the CETA agencies. There are other lesser known agencies which maintain job listings, such as professional associations; you find ways to discover and use them in this chapter.

Chapter 5, "Information Sources about Careers, Industries, Companies," is a compendium of the written information essential to your successful career search and job campaign. In addition to the services of the library, the Better Business Bureaus and Chambers of Commerce of most cities are valuable sources of data about local economics, living conditions, and business activities. The Portland Chamber of Commerce maintains a series of brochures about the local area which you can obtain from the downtown office. The Multnomah County Library, as you see in this chapter, is not just a bunch of bookstacks. Also here you will find an annotated bibliography of 62 books, directories, magazines, newspapers, and encyclopedias which can be useful to you in your search. These are both local and national sources, each briefly described so that you can see at a glance whether it is a source which might be helpful.

Chapter 6, "Career Pitfalls You Can Avoid," is an informal look at some of the most common career problems, exemplified by case studies of several people who have experienced successes and failures in their career paths. These people have found it necessary to take steps to change their life patterns; some have floundered in their attempts, while others have been more fortunate in redirecting themselves.

Several of the agencies in the book perform multiple functions and therefore require inclusion in more than one chapter. This problem of cross-referencing is handled in the following manner: All the particular services of an agency are described individually in the appropriate chapter. For example, if an agency offers vocational guidance and testing you find those services described in Chapter 2. If the same agency also offers classes or support services, those are analyzed in Chapter 3. The agency's placement services would be described in Chapter 4, and library services in Chapter 5. The index at the back of the book indicates each place an agency is listed.

Then Plan Your Strategy

Before accepting the help of an individual or agency, you should carefully consider the precise role of professionals in your career search. It is not uncommon for people to find that they have spent money and time on services that were not helpful to them or did not meet their particular needs. For this reason it is critical for you to have a **planned job-hunting strategy.** Even if you are uncertain about what you would like to do professionally, that is itself a minimum strategy. You know that you need to begin with vocational counseling or testing, rather than a vague resume or a list of potential employers whose questions you cannot answer. Or you might know what you want to do and where you would like to do it, but lack the job-finding skills you need in order to communicate your skills to potential employers. In that case you can seek help in refining job-hunting skills. Or you might be perfectly prepared for interviews, but find it difficult to obtain them. In other words, **you need to know what you need!**

Hire the Best Help You Can Find

Once you know the kinds of help you should have, you must decide who can best offer it to you. Again, I cannot overemphasize the importance of **selectively shopping** for these services. Try to eliminate your stereotypes about any of the agencies, and evaluate them by your own criteria. Remember that in this case you are the employer and you have a right to interview them in terms of your own vocational needs. Above all, know precisely what they can and cannot do for you. Below you find a general set of questions you should find useful in evaluating agencies.

• 20

☐ Are you certain you need the service? Have you at least tried to do it yourself?

☐ Can you obtain the service free of charge with only a minor sacrifice? For example, some tests can be taken free if you are willing to give up the plush office and priestly attention of a counselor.

☐ If you decide to pay someone to help you, what is the maximum amount of money you could be charged? Usually this is related to the amount of time you require the service. A fee of $50 an hour has been known to multiply into the four-figure range.

☐ If you elect to undergo vocational testing, what kind and how much counseling will you receive with the tests? Is this a personal or group experience?

☐ What can you tell about an agency or counselor from the written material it produces?

☐ What kind of track record does the agency have? Can you talk to anyone who has used the service?

☐ How long has the agency been in business? How has it changed? What is the nature of the staff? What are their credentials?

☐ Have you compared at least three agencies which claim to provide the same service?

☐ Do you have a general good feeling about the people you will be working with?

☐ Is there a written contract spelling out everyone's responsibilities?

☐ Are there any hidden costs?

☐ Are there any guarantees?

The Portland Job Market

While the following information is interesting, I give it only cursory attention, for two reasons. First, in many cases, your particular job opportunities in a geographic area are **not** reflected in these statistics. If you are a creative job-hunter you should be able to find a place for your skills in any region. Also, most employment statistics do not reflect higher level management jobs or the corresponding entry level positions. Secondly, this kind of data changes rapidly, is not kept up to date, and is not collected uniformly.

It is helpful to know as much about the economy of an area as you can when you are talking to the people who live there and have the power to offer you job leads or other kinds of help. So it is only to give you a superficial feeling for the Portland area economy that the following is presented.

Portland is the 34th largest Standard Metropolitan Statistical Area in the United States with a population of approximately 1,121,000, an increase of 9.9% since 1970. Almost 2,000,000 people live within 100 miles of Portland. The local per capita income in 1976 was $5,432. The economy has shown a healthy improvement, with the Portland Consumer Price Index showing inflation in 1976 at 6.6%, down from 10.3% in 1975. Educationally, the state's average attainment is higher than the national average on both the high school and college levels.

The Portland area is one of the country's leading wholesale and distribution centers, with the largest volume of per capita wholesale trade on the West Coast. In 1975, agriculture was a $4,600,000 industry in Oregon. Over one third of the standing timber resource in the nation is found in the Pacific Northwest. In the Portland Marketing Region alone, forest industries account for 1,000 manufacturing plants.

No one industry employs more than 11% of the work force. The industries having the most impact on the labor market, however, include forest products, electrical equipment, furniture, food processing, fabricated metals, primary metals, machinery, chemicals, transportation equipment, and textiles and apparel.

Portland is known to have a highly diversified economy characterized by many small firms in every industrial category. The employment average in 1976 was 470,800; 31,500 more people were employed in the metropolitan area than in early 1975. The local unemployment figure was reported at 9% in April 1977, which means that 100,000 people are still looking for work. The labor force is comprised of 36% women and 64% men, as compared to the national figure of 38% women and 62% men. The tri-county area has a nonagricultural work force of 443,500 and represents half of the state's work force. The largest employment category is that of wholesale and retail trade, with 115,000 employed. Manufacturing is second with 92,600; services rank third with 85,100; and the government, which has grown the fastest, employs 73,400 people.

With this data in hand and some clear ideas about how to proceed, you should find this book a handy tool in your career hunt. Good luck!

2. Finding a Suitable Career: *Counseling and Testing*

A thorough analysis of the services of both public and private agencies that can help you decide what you want to do with the more than 20,000 hours you spend working.

You can expect to change careers seven times in your life, according to the most recent statistics. Not jobs, mind you, but **careers.** How do you end up in these careers? Why? When? Your decisions do not have to be accidental, for there are many skilled professionals ready to help you.

Career and life planning is rapidly becoming an important professional field in itself. Trained counselors offer advice on the ways you can ensure that your work values and your personal values coincide. To focus on these issues, these professionals can help you tackle some important questions: You must know exactly what you want to do professionally if you are going to land the job you want. You have to be realistic about your abilities and interests and background. These factors, together with your personal values, relate closely to your career setting — or any one of your seven career settings!

• 24

There is an increasing number of avenues leading toward self-awareness in the vocational arena. Vocational tests have been around for a long time; new ones are being developed and the old ones are revised. Self-analysis tools, such as Richard Bolles' "The Quick Job Hunting Map," are popping up. Vocational counseling is found in almost all educational institutions. In short, we are acting upon the fact that we spend from 20,000 to 80,000 hours of our lives involved with our work.

Vocational testing and vocational counseling usually go hand in hand. There are as many different styles of counseling as there are kinds of tests, and the combination you choose should match your career-planning goals. Often, people have a tendency to put too much faith in testing alone, when the fact is that the tests do not offer easy answers. At best, when combined with vocational counseling, they can offer options and indicate directions for further exploration. A competent counselor can help you develop realistic expectations of your testing program. In this light, it is critical to evaluate your counselor before entering into a time-consuming or costly program of career planning.

Portland is fortunate to have a wide range of counseling and testing services. This chapter analyzes those agencies, including the independent services of the community colleges and public agencies. You will also find a listing of private vocational guidance professionals. Their names were obtained initially from the Yellow Pages, and their services were investigated with a phone call and usually a visit. Only those private services which offer genuine vocational guidance, no matter how expensive, are included here.

In many cases, the counseling and testing functions of an agency are supported by groups or workshops to teach you job-finding skills. These support groups, classes, and seminars are found in Chapter 3. Vocational exploration and testing programs that are conducted for groups are also described in Chapter 3.

Most of these career-planning programs use some testing. To help you understand what they are, and how they are used, I have included a list of the most common tests at the end of this chapter, along with a brief explanation of how each functions.

25 •

Career Studies Program of the Life Planning Center [LPC]
Marylhurst Education Center
Marylhurst, Oregon 97036
636-8141
Cost: Sliding scale, $2 to $10 per hour for
       counseling; $3 to $12 per test
Eligibility: No restrictions

The Life Planning Center at Marylhurst is one of four in the country created by a grant from the Kellogg Foundation. It is first and foremost a community service, affiliated with the Marylhurst Education Center. You don't need to register with the college to use these services.

In its broad sense, the Life Planning Center helps adults in the development of what is called a "Career-Life-Learning Plan." The Career Studies Program focuses on specific vocational needs by combining counseling and testing with a series of workshops and classes (see also Chapter 3). The Career Studies Program helps you assess your abilities, interests, work skills, and personal values. Working with counselors, you explore options in education, volunteer work, and paid employment.

• 26

It is important to note here that the counselors at LPC are flexible in terms of the services they suggest for each client. Vocational testing is used only when it seems appropriate; there is a stronger emphasis on counseling and self-assessment.

The first meeting is a goal-setting session and it costs $5. Each hour of counseling after that costs $10, or less, depending on income. However, if you are not making steady progress and meeting goals after five or six sessions, the counselors refer you to other professional agencies or counselors for personal guidance. In other words, counselors at the Life Planning Center are careful to watch for problems that they are not equipped to handle.

If testing is felt to be valuable, a counselor will select the useful ones for each client from this group:

The Strong-Campbell Interest Inventory	$3
Edwards Personal Preference Schedule	$5
GATB	$12
Career Planning Program	$12
California Psychological Inventory	$5
16 Personality Factors	$5
Taylor-Johnson Temperament	$5
Holland's Self-Directed Search	$3

Other materials, such as Richard Bolles' "The Quick Job Hunting Map," are used in some cases.

The significant thing to remember about the Life Planning Center is this: The counselors treat each client as a person with unique needs. In fact, clients are called "consumers" and are respected accordingly.

Clackamas Community College
19600 S. Molalla Avenue
Oregon City, Oregon 97045
656-2631
Cost: $.50 to $2 for tests
Eligibility: No restrictions

Clackamas Community College has earned the reputation as one of the best places to find a vocational testing program combined with professional counseling. Services are available to anyone free, except for the minimal costs of scoring the tests. The mall area of the main campus building houses the Counseling Center, Placement Center, Testing, Job Information Center, and an Employment Opportunity Board.

Geared for people of all ages and occupational interests, the testing and counseling program focuses on presenting choices. Counselors emphasize that tests cannot tell you what you should be doing; rather, they are tools which, when combined with focused counseling, present workable options to career hunters.

These are the tests given in the normal testing program:

Strong-Campbell Interest Inventory	$2
Minnesota Vocational Interest Inventory	$2
GATB Interest Check List	$ .50
Career Assessment Inventory	$2

The Edwards personality tests are also sometimes used informally to determine personality barriers to occupational goals. You may be given other tests as well if the counselor feels they can help you.

When the test results are received, you meet with the counselor to talk about your options. Sometimes further education is recommended; sometimes classes in the area of career exploration are recommended. (See Chapter 3 for a description of the classes offered by Clackamas Community College.) But no one tells you specifically what you should be doing. Instead, you emerge armed with some realistic ideas about your interests and abilities which enable you to explore career options effectively.

• 28

Division of Continuing Education [DCE]
Portland State University
1633 S.W. Park Avenue
Portland, Oregon 97207
229-4825 or toll-free if outside Portland:
[800] 452-1368
Counselor: Bernice Feibleman
Cost: $55 for five tests and counseling
Eligibility: No restrictions

DCE is probably best known for the classes in career search and job readiness it conducts (see Chapter 3), but this same agency also works with individuals to administer a series of five vocational tests. This program is standard for each person. When you call for an appointment, Ms. Feibleman explains the procedure and schedules the tests.

Your first visit to the DCE office is a counseling/testing session. Ms. Feibleman administers one of the tests; you are then put in a room by yourself for two or three hours to take the other four tests. Since some of these must be sent away to be scored, it is approximately two weeks before you return to meet with Ms. Feibleman for the test interpretation and goal-setting session. If you are fortunate to have fairly consistent test results, this session can be very short. In a few cases, she makes referrals to other agencies, since personal difficulties sometimes prevent the realization of career goals. These are the only two counseling sessions.

The following tests are included in the DCE program:

Strong-Campbell Interest Inventory
Kuder Personal Preference Record
Ammons Quick Test
Adjective Check List
Work Values Inventory

29 •

The combined cost for the tests and counseling sessions is $55.

Ms. Feibleman is also the public relations person for the DCE program, and she is happy to answer questions about it. She is concerned that people realize that it is not designed just for students of PSU or geared exclusively toward women. She feels strongly about the need for self-awareness in the career field. She states, "Most people can achieve a goal on their own, but many need information and knowledge about resources to make a choice."

Mt. Hood Community College
26000 S.E. Stark
Gresham, Oregon 97030
• 30   **667-7461**
Cost: None
Eligibility: No restrictions, with the
exception of the Job Placement
Center, which maintains job
listings for students.

The Counseling Center at Mt. Hood is staffed with vocational counselors who can administer the GATB or the Strong-Campbell Interest Inventory. However, these tests are not always warranted; there is an initial counseling session to determine their suitability. The Counseling Center also houses the Career Information System computer program. You use an instruction manual, interacting with the computer and answering directed questions. The computer leads you through a career path, resulting in a cluster of possible careers which you might then explore.

Mt. Hood also offers a Career Resource Center, containing information about specific occupations, pay scales, employment forecasts, and resume writing. People in the Center can direct you to other services on campus, such as financial aid, placement, counseling, and tutoring. Here you can also find materials to help you with your career hunting. These materials include job experience kits, occupational tapes, the Kuder Interest Test, the California Occupational Guide, and the C.I.S. Needlesort. The Needlesort is a version of the computer program found in the Counseling Center.

The actual placement services of the Job Placement Center are available only to students. However, there is a job board you can watch, and a computer terminal with listings from the Oregon State Employment Service.

The Oregon State Employment Service
1407 S.W. Fourth
Portland, Oregon 97201
229-5005
Cost: None
Eligibility: No restrictions

The State Employment Service offers a broad range of services and a large staff to help clients. In addition to counseling and testing (described here), you can find placement services (see Chapter 4) and special job-finding workshops (see Chapter 3).

The Counseling and Testing Unit is staffed with professional counselors who administer aptitude rather than interest tests. The placement counselor to whom you are assigned when you first come in to the Employment Service must refer you to the testing unit. There are a few two-person teams of placement and testing counselors who work together to solve vocational problems. At the time of this writing, the team concept is in the experimental stage.

This office uses a two-part testing procedure called SEARCH. You take the GATB and the Worker Trait Group Inventory, a checklist. These tests take about three hours. A week later, you receive a computer printout. Then, the second step, you are asked to complete a series of worksheets. These result in a self-selected list of occupations which might interest you. There is a final counseling session with a counselor to determine the kinds of jobs you should be looking for, with the help of a placement counselor.

Sometimes these tests indicate a need for more sophisticated tests. You are then referred to Clackamas Community College to take the Strong-Campbell Interest Inventory and the Edwards Personal Preference Schedule.

Although no personal counseling is performed by the staff at the Employment Service, counselors sometimes find that personal problems are responsible for a client's unemployability. This person would be referred to other family service agencies which can augment the efforts of the Employment Service.

• 32

The counseling unit also maintains a small library filled with local labor statistics and resources. Feel free to ask if you can snoop around in there to learn more about your field.

Portland Community College [PCC]
Sylvania Campus: 12000 S.W. 49th
Portland, Oregon 97219
244-6111
Cost: None
Eligibility: No restrictions

Like the other community colleges, PCC accepts referrals from outside agencies to do vocational testing. There are eight campuses of PCC, but the largest career office is at Sylvania, where a Career Information Center and a Counseling and Testing facility are housed. Counselors can help with learning problems, study skills, career development and exploration, assessment of interests and abilities, and personal or social problems.

No appointments are necessary if you are interested in talking with a counselor. It is a walk-in center. However, you might be wise to call in advance to insure that adequate staffing will be there when you are.

The Career Information System computer search is available, as are several tests to assess vocational interests and abilities. These tests include:

Strong-Campbell Interest Inventory
Kuder Personal Preference Record

Differential Aptitude Test
Edwards Personal Preference Schedule

Other personality and intelligence tests are administered 33 •
if the counselor thinks they might help you.

The Job Placement Center located at the Sylvania
campus offers some valuable services to students, including job-finding advice, resume preparation, video feedback
of interview techniques, and, of course, job placement with
local industries and companies.

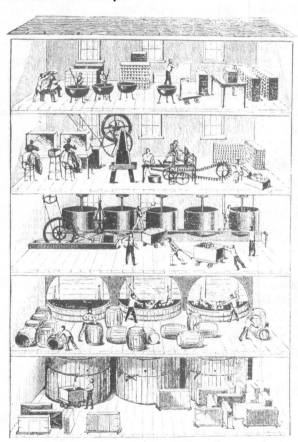

PRIVATE VOCATIONAL GUIDANCE SERVICES

• 34

**Dr. Clarence Colwell, Marriage, Family,
and Child Counselor
1850 S.W. Midvale Road
Portland, Oregon 97219
635-3061
Cost: $35 per 50-minute session
Eligibility: No restrictions**

Dr. Colwell performs vocational counseling and testing in terms of an individual's total life situation. He uses a few tests, but doesn't rely heavily on them; he believes that informal verbal interviewing is a more revealing way to look at a person's life context.

If you are interested solely in vocational counseling and testing, Dr. Colwell is likely to refer you to the community colleges.

**J. Frederick Marcy & Associates, Inc. [JFM]
720 S.W. Washington, Suite 525
Portland, Oregon 97205
222-4244
Managing Director: Curtis H. [Pat] Patterson
Associate Director: Ray Kevane
Cost: Variable, depending on services and
length of program. Fees are set at the
professional rate of $50 an hour; basic
testing and limited counseling: $100-$150.
Eligibility: No restrictions**

Mr. Patterson calls the service a "Total Help Actualization Center" staffed with career consultants. The Marcy organization specializes in people with major redirectional problems; for example, the educator or military person leaving their familiar structure for a new environment, a business executive changing industries or going into self-employment, or a housewife who wants to enter or return to a professional life.

The initial interview at Marcy is free and lasts about one hour. This session delineates specific career problems, and the ways Marcy may be able to help. Costs for further services are set in advance.

Testing is essential here. You take a series of tests developed by JFM called a "Personal Vocational Inventory Profile." These are followed by approximately three hours of counseling, in which you determine focus areas. The testing is designed to assess your feelings, needs, personal variables, and functional traits. This process costs between $100 and $150, depending on the scope of the counseling. You then decide if you want to continue to work with JFM, and, if so, what your program with them will involve.

Counseling can be for both individuals and groups; of course, the individual counseling is more expensive, but group sessions are used to resolve communication problems and common marketing difficulties. The duration of the program is variable; it can last from one week to sixty days.

You should note that JFM cannot, by Oregon law, represent you to any potential employers. It is not an employment agency, is not subject to the state licensing requirements, and therefore cannot arrange employment interviews for you.

The J. Frederick Marcy & Associates brochure depicts the JFM process. From the brochure:

"[The Marketing Program] involves consultations with a professional marketing director, using the information in the credentials we have prepared and centered on: (1) definition of feasible vocational objectives; (2) a complete marketing strategy tailored to your unique needs and goals and implemented with speed and dispatch in the marketplace.''

If this agency sounds a bit esoteric to you, I suggest you check it out carefully. I might mention that I know two men who changed careers with the help of the local JFM consultants. They are both happy in their new jobs. One man paid $1200 for his new happiness; the other, $1000.

Persona Corporation/The Psychology Center
521 S.W. Clay
Portland, Oregon 97201
228-0271 or 227-5425
Clinical Psychologists: Dr. Norman Hickman
                              and Dr. Michael Fleming
Cost: $200
Eligibility: No restrictions

These two psychologists administer a battery of tests, choosing from personality tests, intelligence tests, and vocational tests. They are reluctant to specify which tests are used because they vary with individual cases.

The first counseling session is an orientation; you talk with the psychologists to determine areas in which you need clarification. The testing follows this session and may take as long as a day and a half. There is a final counseling session for test interpretation and vocational goal-setting. Sometimes, biofeedback sessions may be recommended for the client. These are offered at a cost of $20 per session.

This particular process is comparably expensive and may be most useful to experienced professionals who are having directional problems. Feel free to ask if you can talk to Dr. Hickman or Dr. Fleming about the Center before you hire them. When you pay this amount of money for services, you need to be very clear about exactly what you will get.

Dr. Max Reed, Clinical Psychologist
6201 S.W. Capitol Hwy.
Portland, Oregon 97201
246-6966
Cost: $50 per hour
Eligibility: No restrictions

Dr. Reed is a vocational expert for the Bureau of Hearings and Appeals of the federal Department of Health, Education and Welfare, and a consultant to the Departments of Vocational Rehabilitation and Social Security. Fifteen percent of his private practice as a psychotherapist concerns vocational counseling and testing; he helps people who are planning careers in the upper and mid-professional levels such as lawyers, biologists, and nurses.

He works on the premise that vocational or motivational problems might be related to personal problems. For example, you might be having trouble delineating career goals because of minor depression. Dr. Reed uses four types of testing: simple manual dexterity tests, personality tests, intelligence tests, and the Strong-Campbell Interest Inventory. The tests take three hours, followed by a couple of counseling sessions to determine vocational directions. If there are no psychological barriers, this process takes about five hours. The cost for this average procedure, then, would be $250.

• 38

COMMON VOCATIONAL TESTS

As promised, here's a rundown on the various tests you may encounter along the way.

Adjective Check List. By checking off adjectives, you describe yourself, from "absent-minded" to "zany." This measures your needs, personal adjustment, counseling readiness, confidence, and self-control.

Ammons Quick Test. This is a vocabulary test, using a list of words in reference to a set of drawings.

California Psychological Inventory. You check 480 true-false statements, designed to measure your personality traits in relation to your social interactions.

Career Assessment Inventory [CAI]. As a multiple-choice career interest questionnaire, the CAI compares your interests to those of people working in a variety of occupations.

C.I.S. [Career Information System] and C.I.S. Needlesort: This provides current labor market and educational information to improve career choices and training opportunities. It is used also to develop counseling and instructional programs.

Career Planning Program. The CPP evaluates your vocational interests, experience and background, and abilities (mechanical, numerical, spatial, language, and clerical).

Differential Aptitude Test. This one tests your abilities in reasoning, math, verbal, and manual areas.

Edwards Personal Preference Schedule. Interrelated and independent normal personality variables are measured by this test.

GATB [General Aptitude Test Battery]. Counselors call this the best validated multiple aptitude battery. It measures intelligence, and verbal, spatial, mathematical, motor, and manual dexterity.

Holland's Self-Directed Search. Sixteen pages of self-assessment evaluate occupations by six dimensions: Realistic, investigative, artistic, social, enterprising, and conventional. This is a take-home tool; a counselor need never see it.

Kuder Personal Preference Record. Interests are assessed in these five areas: Group activity, stability, preference for working with ideas, avoiding conflict, and directing others.

Minnesota Vocational Interest Inventory. This is designed to measure the interests of nonprofessional men and others interested in trade careers.

16 PF [Sixteen Personality Factors]. You need 45 minutes to take this personality assessment. By answering 187 questions you are described in terms of 16 personality variables, showing those which most influence your life.

- 40 **Strong-Campbell Interest Inventory.** Occupational groups are identified by comparing your interests with those of other people in occupations. This helps you understand how your personal preferences fit into the work world.

Taylor-Johnson Temperament Analysis. This one assesses emotions for individual and marital counseling. It tests personality variables and feelings about yourself.

Work Values Inventory. It is designed to show you the most important factors in your work environment.

Worker Trait Group Inventory. This is a personal interest checklist designed to work with the GATB.

3. Learning Job-Finding Skills

A look at classes, seminars, support groups, and workshops which can teach you a second set of essential skills—how to go about looking for a job, and the tools you need.

Knowing precisely what you want to do with yourself is the most important part of your career plan. But it's not a job. Now you have to go job-hunting; you have to send out resumes and track down influential people and perform well in job interviews. In other words, you need another set of skills—job-finding skills—in addition to the skills you have already acquired to actually do that job.

In this chapter you find analyses of seminars, work-shops, support groups, and classes designed to help you through. Some of them can help you with technical problems such as resume preparation and interview techniques. Others teach you the tricks of job-hunting — the kinds of communication skills you need, the different ways you can use resumes, follow-up procedures, and other important aspects of getting the job you want.

Perhaps you might feel more comfortable exploring career options together with other career hunters. A lot of vocational counseling and testing is done in classes and group workshops. The community colleges offer career exploration classes to the public. The State Employment Service offers a program of group testing and counseling. There are others, described in this chapter.

Professional resume preparation services included here are designed to provide you with a resume painlessly. But you should carefully consider the pros and cons of using professionally prepared resumes.

You will note that many of the organizations in this chapter are also mentioned elsewhere in this book. That's because many of the agencies in Portland offer distinct but related programs. Their counseling and testing services were outlined in Chapter 2, and their classes and follow-up services are described here.

In the same way, some of the agencies in Chapter 4 also provide support services to their clients. For example, CETA is the federal entity blessed with the task of solving some difficult unemployment problems; therefore the CETA agencies are analyzed in Chapter 4. But they also conduct employment workshops for their clients. The same is true of the Apprenticeship Information Center; the counselors there provide support and counseling throughout the selection process.

43 •

So now that you know what you want to do with yourself, decide whether you might need some help learning how to find that job.

Career Studies Program of the Life Planning Center
Marylhurst Education Center
Marylhurst, Oregon 97036
636-8141
Cost: $30 per credit hour [except where
noted otherwise]
Eligibility: No restrictions

In addition to the vocational exploration services of the Life Planning Center (see Chapter 2), the Career Studies Program offers courses for career hunters.

• **Life Career Planning for Men and Women.** Instructor: Joseph Dubay. 2 credit hours.
Designed for people thinking about the next steps in their lives, this course can help with the decision-making process. The focus is goal-setting, confidence-building, tools for career choice, resource discovery, and self-directed change.

- **Pre-Retirement Workshop.** Instructors: Marcia Hoyt and Joseph Dubay. Cost: $30 for individuals, $45 for couples. Many people never think about how they will live when they retire. This class helps people of all ages begin retirement planning.

• 44

- **Being Male Today.** Instructors: David Judd and Roger Bishop. 1 credit hour.
  A five-session class, this series is designed to help men learn to deal with the changing roles and new directions of women.

- **Creative Choices for Women.** Instructors: Marcia Hoyt, Trudy Wallace, and Jan Wetzel. 3 credit hours. Cost: $97.50, including testing fees.
  This class concerns areas of both identity and direction, covering awareness of role behavior, values, decision-making, and skill assessment. Teaching methods include small group work as well as personality, aptitude and interest testing. One individual counseling session is included. The focus of the class is to examine opportunities in paid and non-paid employment, and education options.

Other classes in the Career Studies Program include:

"Assertiveness Training I and II"
"Marriage Enrichment"
"Introduction to Bioenergenics"
"Parenting: Exploring Dilemmas and Delights"
"Women as Winners"

Clackamas Community College
19600 S. Molalla Avenue
Oregon City, Oregon 97045
656-2631
Cost: $12 per credit hour, $8 per credit hour
to audit
Eligibility: No restrictions

Clackamas Community College is well known for its counseling and vocational testing programs (see Chapter 2). This good reputation is equally deserved for the classes and workshops in career exploration.

• **Career Planning.** Instructor: Norm Berney. 1 credit hour.
Although listed as a psychology course, the class is taught by one of the school's vocational counselors. It gives students a personal look at different occupations and career fields. Comparable to most career planning workshops, the class focuses on assessment of personal values, to help determine which vocational choices fit into a total life plan.

• **Job Search Techniques.** Instructors: Marv Thornly and Dolly Ammons. 1 credit hour.
This course is required of all students enrolled in vocational programs at the college. It explores the basics of job-hunting, including what to look for in a job, resume preparation, sources of information about jobs and careers, and interviewing preparation and practice.

• **Focus on Women.** Instructors: Bernice Evans and Bernie Nolan.
An on-going program, these seminars help women who have initial or reentry problems with the work world. The workshops cover different topics, including

self-analysis, testing, and other aspects of career exploration. One or two monthly sessions last one hour, and the cost is $1 per session. For further information contact the Counseling Department and ask for Ms. Evans or Ms. Nolan.

• **Career Development and College Success.** Instructors: Vincent Fitzgerald, Bernice Evans, and Bernie Nolan. 3 credit hours.

This class has been designed for people who, because of absence from formal education or the work world, have a low level of general skills and achievement. It offers overviews of math, English, and reading skills, while attempting to boost the self-image of people before they take on a curriculum or job.

Division of Continuing Education
Portland State University
1633 S.W. Park
Portland, Oregon 97201
229-4825, or toll-free outside Portland: 1-800-452-1268
Cost: Varies, depending on class
Eligibility: No restrictions

In addition to conducting an on-going counseling and vocational testing program (see Chapter 2), Bernice Feibleman coordinates a series of classes for people interested in learning job-finding skills.

- **Charting New Directions.** Cost: $32.50 for each workshop; lunch included.
   This is a series of three one-day workshops aimed at women who are ready for a change in jobs, education, or other areas. Vocational testing is combined with group counseling to examine decision-making and goal-setting.

- **It's Your Career.** Cost: $90 with 1 hour of credit; $75 without credit.
   This is a five-session counseling and testing workshop for employed men and women. The workshop examines career decisions, resumes, and interviewing techniques. Some individual counseling is also included.

- **Job Readiness.** Cost: $30 without credit; $35 with 2 credit hours.
   A series of six classes designed for women preparing to return to work. Moderators and speakers examine employment techniques and alternatives, places to locate jobs, and job-finding skills. Each of the six days features an aspect of the job search: resume preparation, interviews, goal-setting, and strategies.

The Employment Orientation Program
1010 Washington
Vancouver, Washington 98660
• 48   **[206] 694-8452**
Director: Beverly Fogel, Trend Systems, Inc.
Cost: None
Eligibility: Washington residents only

Trend Systems, Inc. has a contract with the state government to offer employment orientation to Washington residents in Vancouver, Olympia, Spokane, Yakima, and Kenowick. It is a 40-hour workshop, four hours a day for ten weekdays. Touching all phases of the job search, the program has been successful in helping people of all ages and educational levels find jobs. It is designed for career changers, housewives, skilled and unskilled workers and people who are tired of retirement.

Classes of 15 to 18 people cover several areas of job-finding skills. First, members learn how to make decisions about career paths. There is no formal testing program, but informal techniques are used as they are needed. Then you explore the ways to research jobs and companies. You practice writing resumes, job descriptions, cover letters, and applications. Emphasis is on learning effective communication skills. Students learn interview techniques primarily by the use of role playing. The program covers all the important little points—how to get past secretaries, nonverbal communication, timing, and the red flags you should watch for in job-hunting.

There is a 60-day follow-up service, and you can use the program as a support system during your actual job hunt.

The "HELP!" Program
Mt. Hood Community College
26000 S.E. Stark
Gresham, Oregon 97030
667-1561
Director: Maxine Watson
Cost: None
Eligibility: No restrictions, but
          specialization in helping single
          or unemployed heads of
          households.

"HELP!" is a grant project in the Consumer Homemaking category of the State Department of Education. Anyone is welcome to drop in to the open classroom between 9:00 a.m. and noon Mondays, Wednesdays, and Fridays.

Ms. Watson runs the program very informally. The focus of the project is to teach group members how to manage their personal resources, such as time and money. It also serves as a resource for career exploration; you can learn how to prepare for a job search, improve self-confidence through assertion training, and assess skills and personal values. Relationships with others are explored, with a strong emphasis on improving communication and listening skills. Some testing, including the Strong-Campbell Interest Inventory and the Career Information Search, is also provided. There is always free babysitting, and an emphasis on working mothers relating to the needs of their children.

**Jobs for Veterans Program/National
Alliance of Businessmen [NAB]
Portland Metro Office**

• 50   **921 S.W. Washington
Portland, Oregon 97205
226-4063
Manager, Jobs for Veterans: Chuck Long
Cost: None
Eligibility: Vietnam-era veterans**

Chuck Long conducts a monthly Veteran Employment Seminar Program (VESP). The three-hour program is free to veterans and covers sources of jobs and counseling, resume preparation, benefits available to veterans, employment alternatives, and job interview strategies. Mr. Long reports that these seminars are effective in helping veterans find jobs.

The National Alliance of Businessmen is not a job-finding agency per se, but is instrumental in creating an environment where hard-to-hire groups of people receive stronger considerations in hiring. Headquartered in Washington, D.C., NAB has more than 130 local offices. It is a nonprofit organization of people from business, government, education, and labor, combining resources to focus on unemployment. Its funding is one-fourth federal; the rest comes from private industry donations.

The following five groups are the focus of the NAB promotional efforts: Vietnam-era veterans, handicapped or disabled veterans, ex-offenders, economically disadvantaged people, and young people. These groups traditionally have severe unemployment problems even when the economy is flourishing. NAB does not provide job placement, but works closely with the State Employment Service and local employers.

Labor Education Advancement Program [LEAP]
Urban League of Portland
5329 N.E. Union Avenue
Portland, Oregon 97211
288-6361
Cost: None
Eligibility: No restrictions

LEAP is a federally funded organization founded eight years ago to help minorities; the Women's Division was added two years ago. It primarily serves people who aspire to union careers, covering trades from auto mechanic to steamfitter to steelworker.

The Women's Division is headed by Margaret Solomon, Recruiter Counselor. She helps women who are interested in both traditional and nontraditional jobs, but her basic concern is that women do not end up in dead-end jobs. The Men's Division is staffed by Terry Williamson, Recruiter Counselor, and Paul Rhemus, Tradesman Specialist.

The procedure for someone interested in a trade career is this: You work with the LEAP counselors to decide which trades might be best for you, then you visit the Apprenticeship Information Center (see Chapter 4), then you go before the Joint Apprenticeship Committee where you are assessed and placed.

LEAP provides a support system as you go through this process, counseling you about trades, and helping you prepare for the GATB or other tests. Once you are accepted into a trade, LEAP can provide continuous tutorial and support services. Other services include an employment office with a job order book with more traditional jobs. There is never a fee for any of these services.

• 52

Eugene Montrose and Associates
P.O. Box 521
Portland, Oregon 97207
238-7108
Cost: $50 per hour for group counseling
Eligibility: No restrictions

Mr. Montrose is a public relations and legislative consultant to the Oregon Private School Association. He no longer works with individuals on a counseling basis, but refers people to vocational schools in any area of the country free of charge. He can perform counseling on a group basis, if you want to assemble a group of people and share his fee of $50 an hour. He estimates that he can do a thorough job with a group in five meetings of two hours each. His counseling covers what you want to do in your job, the kinds of companies to look for, the sales techniques that work in job interview situations, and resume writing. The only individual counseling he does regularly is with deaf and blind job-hunters.

Mt. Hood Community College
26000 S.E. Stark
Gresham, Oregon 97030
667-1561
Cost: $12 to $14 per credit hour
Eligibility: No restrictions

In addition to its counseling and testing services (see Chapter 2), Mt. Hood offers classes to help people discover and implement career goals. The cost of classes is determined by the number of credit hours; you pay $12 per credit hour if you live in the Mt. Hood district, and $14 per credit hour if you live outside the district.

• **Career and Life Planning.** Instructor: Robert Kull. 3 credit hours.

Mr. Kull uses "The Quick Job Hunting Map" by Richard Bolles and the GATB to help students look at career fields in light of their personal values and goals. The class helps clarify values and assess interests, needs, attitudes, skills, abilities, and lifestyles. Students become familiar with resources on campus and in the community. Small groups and interviews are used to find patterns of likes and dislikes.

• **Creative Job Search.** Instructor: Robert Kull. 2 credit hours.

Most of the students in this class know what they want to do. "Go Hire Yourself An Employer" by Richard Irish is used to show nontraditional ways to approach the job market. As a student in the class you (1) assess what you can offer an employer, (2) try to define your ideal job, (3) learn how to use a resume and cover letter, (4) learn the resources available to help research companies, and (5) learn how to use informational interviewing to contact companies and key personnel.

Oregon State Employment Service
1407 S.W. Fourth
Portland, Oregon 97201
• 54   **229-5005**
Cost: None
Eligibility: No restrictions

In addition to the placement services (see Chapter 4) and the vocational counseling and testing services (see Chapter 2), the State Employment service offers workshops to help job-hunters. You must be referred to these groups by a placement counselor.

• **Job Finding Workshop.**
This workshop is one session, every other Wednesday from 9:00 a.m. to noon. It serves no special age or occupational group; rather, anyone can attend for help in organizing a job search, handling interviews, using resumes, finding job information sources, and more. A special resume kit and resume guide are used in the workshop. Appointments should be made at the information desk or by calling the counseling and testing unit at 229-5641.

• **Job Opportunities Exploration [JOE].**
Five sessions are scheduled in two weeks, covering skills assessment, interests, abilities, and the total job search. Each session concentrates on a particular aspect of the career-finding process: (1) orientation and preparation for testing; (2) testing, including GATB and the Worker Trait Inventory; (3) test interpretation (this process is called SEARCH); (4) skills assessment and a personal work analysis; and (5) a job/career search and an employability plan. On-going counseling sessions can be arranged for Friday afternoons if clients are interested in continuing

support. Appointments for the JOE program can be made by calling 229-5641.

- **The Tuesday-Thursday Group.** Conducted by Manpower instructors.

    This group serves experienced, mature professionals. It consists of one session, with twelve people in a group. It is primarily a resource seminar to explore directories and trade journals, as well as to organize a job search. This seminar does a good job of addressing the problems of job-hunting etiquette—how to dress for an interview, how to offer follow-up contacts, etc. The seminar also works as a group intake for the computerized job match. The procedure is tedious and lends itself well to group work. Further information about the Tuesday-Thursday group is available from the information desk.

- **People for Jobs.** Published by the State Employment Service.

    It includes mini-profiles of job hunters and is sent to approximately 800 Portland employers. The mini-resumes are also broadcast on Channel 6 Monday at noon, and on ten radio stations.

- **The Jobs Hot Line, 248-WORK.**

    A recorded list of first-day job orders as they are sent to the State Employment Service. Fresh listings are received at 8:30 a.m. and at 5:00 p.m., and the recorded message runs 24 hours a day, seven days a week.

Portland Community College
Main campus: Sylvania
12000 S.W. 49th
Portland, Oregon 97219
244-6111
Eligibility: No restrictions

There is currently only one class designed to help people explore career options and learn job-finding strategies. However, the Community Education program encourages instructors to hold evening career search classes. It might pay to watch the upcoming course offerings.

• **Career Development.** Instructor: Anne Clarkson. Cost: $38.25. 3 credit hours.
A two-part psychology course, "Career Development" helps you make career choices. You explore work values, abilities, interests, and feelings as they relate to career alternatives. Exercises in communication skills, self-understanding, decision-making, and information-gathering help you relate to your work as a conscious choice.

Portland State University Career Planning
and Placement Office
University Services Building, Room 402
617 S.W. Montgomery
Portland, Oregon 97207
229-4613
Cost: None
Eligibility: 1. Portland State University students
2. Graduates of nonlocal universities
3. Anyone with 12 or more credits at PSU
4. Summer program open to the community

The Career Planning and Placement Office offers a summer "Employment Preparation Program" to anyone in the community free of charge. This summer program covers the same material available to students during the rest of the year.

Four seminars which are continually open to students are Resume Preparation, Resume Critiques, Interviewing, and Job Search Sources.

The Career Resource Center contains tons of information about the Portland area, including employer information, annual reports, house organs, and job descriptions. There are Affirmative Action registers, Bureau of Labor reports, and special files for teachers, government, and medical job hunters. The librarian is in the Center on Mondays, Tuesdays, and Wednesdays. Students also can sign up for interviews via a recruiting calendar of companies visiting the campus.

Women in New and Non-Traditional
Employment Roles [WINNER]
National Organization for Women [NOW]
235-2549

WINNER is a local group of women employed in traditionally male jobs. They maintain a speaker's bureau and hold monthly meetings where women get together to talk about job-related problems.

I went to a meeting of WINNER. There were eight women in occupations such as water engineer, probation officer, lumber trader, and phone lineman. The atmosphere was friendly and informal.

There is also a local NOW Employment Task Force. The name of the person in charge of this can be obtained by calling the local chapter. Or you can write the national task force: NOW Labor Task Force, 520 Butternut Street, N.W., Washington, D.C. 20012.

The Women's Resource Center at the YWCA
1111 S.W. Tenth
Portland, Oregon 97205
• 58　**223-6281 [ext. 67 and 70]**
Director: Anne Fraser Bagwell
Cost: None
Eligibility: No restrictions, but specializes
in nontraditional jobs for both
men and women.

Through the Women's Resource Center (which is for men, too!), the YWCA is developing a program of career and life-planning seminars. They also have a job readiness workshop which focuses on resume preparation, interviewing skills, and assessment of personal values. New programs and services are being developed constantly; feel free to call the YWCA for details.

RESUME PREPARATION SERVICES

You might decide you don't need a resume at all. Several job-finding strategists recommend against it, for a variety of reasons. You decide for yourself, using the job strategy you have laid out. If you decide you don't need a resume, you have saved yourself considerable time, or perhaps money.

If you feel you do need a resume, chances are you will decide to write it yourself. This is a long process; in fact, it never ends. I remember reading that there is no such thing as the perfect resume. It always need revision. I don't mean to sound discouraging—a good resume is a fun challenge. When you work on your resume, try to envision it as a sales brochure for your abilities. That will prompt you to get away from traditional forms. There is nothing that says your resume must follow some of those boring old formats.

When you are deciding how to approach the resume

question, consider this: Many employers claim they can identify a resume which has been professionally prepared; they say it reeks of perfection and impersonality.

Nevertheless, you may have reason for hiring someone to write your resume for you. In that case, be sure to investigate anyone whose services you might buy. Portland does not have an abundance of resume preparation services, but there is variety among the three I discovered:

Bee Office Services
4627 N.E. Fremont
Portland, Oregon 97213
284-2646
Susie Hordichok
Cost: $35 for composition and 25 copies of a
    two-page resume
    $3.50 to type a resume which is
    already prepared
Eligibility: No restrictions

You must visit the office to complete an information form which covers your experience, education, skills, interests, and other relevant information. Ms. Hordichok uses this information to select the appropriate format for your resume. She tries to keep most resumes to two pages. The procedure usually takes two days.

Career Coordinators
1208 S.W. 13th
Portland, Oregon 97205
228-7083
Daryl and Sandra Fleck
Cost: Variable; average cost for 25 copies of
    a two-page resume is $35
Eligibility: No restrictions

Other divisions:

Professional Resume Service	Professional Resume Service
1208 S.W. 13th, Suite 204	13721 S.E. Lincoln
Portland, Oregon 97204	Portland, Oregon 97236
228-4100	255-6601

The resume service is coupled with minor counseling regarding cover letters, resources, places to try to find jobs, and how to use resumes. You must visit the office and fill out an information form. The Flecks go over this form with you, assessing your personality and background to get an idea of how to pursue the resume. The formats are individualized; only rarely do they use a standard one. The length of the resume varies, but is usually under two pages. Career Coordinators also edits and prints resumes; the cost for these services varies, depending on the state of the resume when you bring it to them.

Nationwide Resume Service
2104 S.E. Tamarack
Portland, Oregon 97214
235-5582
Ralph Irwin
Cost: Variable, starting at $25 for 50 printed copies
Eligibility: No restrictions

Mr. Irwin's background is that of a technical writer; he currently writes resumes in many different styles and types. On an interview basis, he evaluates your needs and background. From this conversation he writes a rough draft of your resume and goes over it with you to make revisions and clear up shady areas. The process usually takes two or three days. The cost varies, depending on the services outlined in the initial meeting.

4. Immediate Job Access: *Where to Find Local Job Listings*

An outline of traditional placement services, government agencies, and employment agencies...as well as nontraditional avenues you may not have considered.

Let's assume that your career plan is complete. You know what you want to do, you know where you want to live, you are happy with your resume, and you think you present yourself well. All you need, then, are job interviews.

It's common knowledge that today's job market is a buyer's market; employers can pick and choose who they want to work for them. Job stability is becoming a thing of the past. Workers are often replaced if someone better comes along, or they quit in pursuit of a better position; and employers aren't always careful in screening applicants, so employees are occasionally ill-suited to their jobs.

According to popular rumor, eighty percent of the jobs filled each year are never advertised. No one even knows they exist until suddenly there is a new face in the office. These jobs are filled from the ranks of relatives, friends, friends of friends, or unusually enterprising job-hunters.

However, this chapter concerns the other twenty percent of the publicly offered job opportunities, positions for which employers seek people to meet specific needs.

In Portland there are more job sources than you would expect. Of course, the employment agencies, together with government employment bureaus, are the first organizations most people turn to when they need a job. But there are also professional associations with placement bureaus which, while unable to function as employment agencies, can match employers with job-hunters. Other independent agencies operate on nonprofit bases or as offshoots of governmental agencies. Don't hesitate to use these sources to land jobs which, while not exactly what you want, buy you time to do a thorough job of career and life planning.

Here are places to look in Portland when you must have a job, or have opted to pursue job-hunting in this traditional way. This chapter includes agencies which maintain job listings, the State Employment Service (placement services only), the civil service commissions, professional associations, CETA, employment agencies, and temporary employment services.

GOVERNMENT AGENCIES

The Apprenticeship Information Center [AIC]
A public service of the Oregon State
  Employment Service
1437 S.W. Fourth
Portland, Oregon 97201
229-6080
Cost: None
Eligibility: No restrictions

63 •

Counselors provide general and specific information about apprenticeships and trade careers. They outline the qualifications for trades, helping you determine which ones are best suited to your interests and abilities. Then they guide you through the selection process, offering counseling and support.

When you enter the AIC office, someone talks to you about the trades that interest you, and discusses the ones which currently are open for apprentice positions. If vocational testing seems necessary, the counselor schedules the tests for you through the State Employment Service. Once you have selected a trade, AIC checks the book of standards for the minimum qualifications for that trade. The counselors can show you avenues for meeting those qualifications quickly. You are then scheduled to appear before a Joint Apprenticeship Committee, comprised of three employers and three journeymen in the trade. They assess your interests and background. Here, particularly, it is to your advantage to research the field carefully; the committee is watching for interest and motivation. If you pass, you are placed on an eligibility list, controlled by the committee. It is the committee that places you into an apprenticeship position. If you do not pass the committee assessment, you are encouraged to return to the AIC and apply for a different trade.

The AIC also has a shelf filled with books and journals about trade occupations. Several of these, such as the book of standards, cannot be found in the libraries.

Clackamas Community College
19600 S. Molalla Avenue
Oregon City, Oregon 97045
656-2631
Cost: None
Eligibility: No restrictions

Unlike the other colleges which offer job placement only to their students and alumni, Clackamas Community College offers placement services to anyone in the community. Job listings are posted on a prominent bulletin board, as are regular recruiting schedules of companies visiting the campus looking for talent. To use the service, simply visit the campus, fill out an application, and file your credentials. The office needs to be kept up-to-date on your job-hunting progress, interview results, and current address and phone.

The other community colleges have different requirements for use of their services; it's possible you might qualify—give them a call.

Department of Vocational Rehabilitation,
  State of Oregon
215 S.W. Fourth
Portland, Oregon 97201
229-5050
Director: William Brown
Cost: None
Eligibility: 1. Anyone with a diagnosable
    physical, mental, or emotional
    handicap may be eligible.
  2. The handicap must be
    vocational, as determined by a
    vocational rehabilitation
    counselor.
  3. There must be a reasonable
    expectation that a client will
    be helped by this service.

Not a maintenance or emergency service, this agency accepts referrals from doctors, lawyers, Social Security, corrections, alcohol, and drug programs. A Vocational Evaluation Center can administer tests, or clients are referred to the State Employment Service for assessment. Metropolitan Portland has fourteen field offices with a total staff of 127 people, 70 of them counselors.

In some cases counselors find it necessary to hire independent consultants to help diagnose medical or psychological disabilities. There is a job development staff working with the placement services to guide handicapped people into productive occupations. Although clients sometimes receive help with training or transportation costs, vocational counseling is the critical factor in getting handicapped people into the job market.

• 66

The Oregon State Employment Service
1407 S.W. Fourth
Portland, Oregon 97201
229-5005
Cost: None
Eligibility: No restrictions

The State Employment Service helps a broad range of applicants in several ways (see Chapter 2 for a description of the counseling and testing services, and Chapter 3 for a discussion of workshops and job search services).

Job placement services and referrals are handled in two ways at the State Employment offices:

1. **Microfilm machines** list all job orders. This self-screening process is used to refer most applicants to employers. These are available for use at any time and someone can show you how to use the machine. When you find a job order that interests you, a placement counselor discusses it with you and makes an appointment with the employer. If that job is filled or seems unsuitable, the counselor can help locate other job orders as well as opportunities with other employes.

2. **The computerized job match** is commonly used when applicants have specific skills, training, or professional experience. A placement counselor works with you, finding key words in your field to put into the computer; these words, in turn, match with computerized job orders. When the computer locates a match you are notified by telephone within 12 hours.

Portland Opportunities Industrialization Center [POIC]
5329 N.E. Union
Portland, Oregon 97211
287-1271
Director: Joe Washington
Cost: Variable, depending on program
**   No cost to CETA clients**
Eligibility: CETA, WIN clients; others on a
**   fee basis, with specialization in**
**   serving people with economic,**
**   educational, or social**
**   disadvantages**

67 •

POIC serves the community in two ways:

1. As the City of Portland's Title I CETA training agent, POIC provides prevocational training, on-the-job training, and vocational follow-up. Clients are placed in a work environment and followed through the program. To see how POIC fits into the total CETA picture, read the CETA entry in this chapter (page 73).

2. POIC also operates an independent Clerical Training Program. The program serves WIN and CETA clients, but it is open to anyone. Operated like a business college, the program is geared toward careers in the secretarial and clerical field. Programs are individualized; the program is open entry/open exit. A staff of four counselors assesses clients in all phases of the program. Sometimes clients are referred into an on-the-job training program or placed in jobs through the employment service.

The Women's Resource Center at the YWCA
1111 S.W. Tenth
Portland, Oregon 97205
223-6281 [ext. 67 & 70]
Director: Anne Fraser Bagwell
Cost: None
Eligibility: No restrictions, but specializes
in nontraditional jobs for both
men and women

- 68

Job listings from local employers are still sent to the YWCA from the days when the now-defunct Portland Job Bank was located there. These listings are available to anyone and are supplemented with information about trade apprentice programs. Ms. Bagwell also does career counseling on an appointment basis, together with vocational counselors from Lewis and Clark College. Seminars and workshops are also offered (see Chapter 3).

CIVIL SERVICE CAREERS:
CITY, COUNTY, STATE, FEDERAL

No matter what else we can say about the government, it has a good reputation as an employer. The pay is generally competitive with the private sector, the benefits are excellent, one can be assured of a reasonable degree of job security, and promotions are preferred to hiring outsiders into higher level positions.

Of course, there is the problem of the bureaucracy; the hiring process is often tedious, complicated, and frustrating. The civil service bureaus serve as screening agents. They procure the qualification exams and develop eligibility lists for the agencies which do the actual interviewing and hiring.

The civil services in Portland function independently of each other and differ widely in their procedures. Each is described here in detail.

The City of Portland Civil Service
510 S.W. Montgomery
Portland, Oregon 97201
248-4352
Hotline: 248-4573. A recorded listing of job
openings, 24 hours a day, seven
days a week

Announcements of jobs are posted for a minimum of two weeks, as required by state law. Application forms are tailored to particular job openings, as are the testing procedures. These examinations test for the specific skills required on the job; some are oral while others are written, technical, or manual. An eligibility register is then comprised of those who scored well on the tests.

When a job needs to be filled the names of the top three people on the register are sent to the hiring agency, which interviews them and selects one. If none of these three works out, the next three names are sent. However, the order of names on the list is constantly changing as open competitive exams produce new high scorers. Names remain on the eligible register for one year.

Multnomah County Civil Service
426 S.W. Stark, Seventh Floor
Portland, Oregon 97204
• 70   **248-5035 [recorded information on open**
competitive jobs]
248-5015 [regular business]

Jobs are posted for two weeks on an announcement board. Unlike the city's bureau, the county civil service application form is standardized. You must fill it out and submit any other materials required for the position, which will be classified in one of four departments: Human Services, Justice Services, Administrative Services, and Environmental Services. If you meet the minimum qualifications you are notified to take the appropriate tests, which may be written, oral, or practical demonstrations. Anyone with a score of 75/100 or better is placed on the eligibility list. Again, the agency with the job opening actually does the interviewing and placement.

The county civil service office also maintains an Affirmative Action Board with a few job listings. If you are interested in working for the county in a position which is not open for application, you are encouraged to fill out a Job Interest Card; you will be notified when a job in that area becomes available.

The State of Oregon Civil Service
1400 S.W. Fifth, Room 136
Portland, Oregon 97201
229-6427

71 •

Like the others, the state's civil service bureau establishes eligibility lists for state agencies. These agencies then interview and do the actual hiring. Two bulletin boards contain job announcements; however, this does not necessarily mean actual positions are currently open. One board contains announcements of Current State Employees Promotional Opportunities; the other contains jobs open to you if you do not already work for the state. You must ask for copies of these announcements at the desk, which describe how to apply for the positions.

There are two application procedures: (1) To apply for positions which do not require written tests, you must complete the standardized application and mail it to the Salem civil service office. You receive a rating by mail which determines your place on the eligibility list. (2) Many positions require written tests which are regularly administered in the Portland office. In this case you bring the application form with you to the test and the whole package is mailed to Salem by the Portland staff. Again, you receive a rating by mail.

Eligibility lists are comprised of the names of the top 15 scorers. There is no way to know if you are on this list; even if you have a high rating, there may be many people with higher ones. Your rating is good for one year. However, if you are unhappy with it, you can apply for a new one in six months (90 days for clerical).

**United States Federal Civil Service Commission
Job Information Center [JIC]
1220 S.W. Third, First floor**

• 72 **Portland, Oregon 97204
221-3141
Regional headquarters are located in Seattle**

The Job Information Center is exactly that. Two huge boards list federal jobs open for applications. Job descriptions can be obtained by asking at the information desk. Application procedures differ for various jobs. For example, sometimes it is necessary to submit an application and then take a test; other times the test precedes the application process. The types of positions, the GS levels, and the application procedures are so variable that you must go to the Job Information Center personally to investigate job areas of interest to you.

Tests are scheduled by the Examiner's Office in the JIC office. If you pass the test, your name is placed on an eligibility list which is kept in the JIC office. Federal agencies request the lists as they need people to interview. Your name remains on the list for one year, but you may retest immediately if you are not happy with your score. If you are interested in federal employment outside the Portland area, the JIC can contact the right office for you and help you with the application process there. If the job you want is not open for application, you can fill out a Job Interest Card which insures that you will be notified when it becomes open.

The federal civil service is complicated, but the people who staff the JIC are helpful and knowledgeable. They try their best to keep the intimidating nature of the federal bureaucracy under control.

THE COMPREHENSIVE EMPLOYMENT
AND TRAINING ACT [CETA]

As one of the federal government's major weapons against unemployment and underemployment, CETA differs from the older War on Poverty programs in one critical aspect: The CETA programs are 100% federally funded, but 100% locally run. The advantage of this, of course, is that officials in each local program can design programs and use funds where they can do the most good.

The federal CETA guidelines are universal. Theoretically. Depending on the specific program (CETA has Titles I through IX), funds are available to help people who are unemployed for a particular period of time, employed in a job below their abilities, or educationally or economically disadvantaged. CETA is intended to aid anyone who is handicapped in the competitive job market.

The Portland area has three CETA programs: the City, Clackamas county, and Washington/Multnomah counties. They differ from each other both in the ways they are administered and in the ways they modify the federal guidelines.

Like most federal agencies, CETA is complicated. What follows here is an overview of the three programs, describing the basic services they can provide. You should feel free to call for more detailed information if you would like it.

The City of Portland CETA Title I Program
522 S.W. Fifth, 6th and 8th Floors
Portland, Oregon 97204
- 74   **248-4710**
Acting Director: Phil McLaurin

Three client groups are served by the city's CETA Title I program: youth, ages 14 to 21; adults, ages 22 to 54; and older workers, over 55 years old. The adult system, described here, is somewhat complicated, but at the same time very functional.

The recruiting, intake, and assessment functions are performed at the Ross Island Center of Portland Community College. All assessment is done there, resulting in an Employability Development Plan (EDP) for each client. An EDP team determines if a client's goals are feasible in terms of funding opportunities and realistic expectations of the job market. Clients are then referred to POIC (see page 67) for training, if needed. All training is done at POIC or is farmed out to other agencies, as determined by the EDP. POIC counselors provide continuous follow-up and counseling. Once training is complete, clients are placed in jobs by employment service counselors and job developers who are subcontracted to CETA. Throughout the training process, clients are paid a stipend, for up to 104 weeks.

Other services offered by the city's Title I program include personal counseling, health care, and transportation. Services for youth and older workers are operated by the CETA program directly and are not subcontracted to other agencies.

The Clackamas County CETA Program
P.O. Box 215
Marylhurst, Oregon 97036
635-4591   75 •
Director: Del Smith

Activities of this CETA agency are centrally administered and integrated, although some services require the use
of outside facilities.

Pretesting is performed by CETA to determine the
extent to which testing is necessary; the testing itself is
done at Clackamas Community College. Employment
workshops at the Clackamas CETA agency include help
with resume writing, career planning, and self-analysis;
moreover, CETA is fortunate to have the use of videotape
feedback machines, valuable tools in learning interviewing
techniques. Clients are not paid to attend these workshops.
Vocational training includes classroom training, work
experience, and on-the-job training. Classroom training is
performed by community colleges, private vocational
schools, and workshops such as those offered through the
Division of Continuing Education. The State Employment
Service provides two job developers for the program.

Personal counseling, medical and dental care, and
transportation services are also offered by CETA.

The Multnomah-Washington CETA Consortium
806 S.W. Broadway
Portland, Oregon 97205
• 76   **248-5192**
Director: John M. Wills

Only a small amount of vocational testing is performed by the CETA consortium; the majority of testing needs are met by the State Employment Service or the community colleges. An Adult Practical Living test is administered by CETA, which attempts to assess the client's general ability to cope with the world.

This CETA agency has had remarkable success in getting people jobs. The reason, they say, is not really clear, but is most likely the fact that they **pay** clients to attend a set of employment workshops. These workshops help people with special employability problems, such as those of women or veterans. Another set of workshops helps unskilled people find entry-level jobs. Everyone is assessed prior to vocational training. CETA uses the community colleges or private vocational schools to provide the training. Actual work programs include a work experience program and an on-the-job training program with private employers.

Day-care services and transportation costs are also provided by the CETA Consortium.

PROFESSIONAL ASSOCIATIONS
AND PLACEMENT BUREAUS

Every field has its own professional organizations. Portland entertains many of them; some are local chapters of national associations, while others are local endeavors.

It's worth taking the time to find the local organizations in your field — they are gathering places for people in the profession. Most have regular meetings you can attend to meet people in the field, hear of job leads, and get your name out. These people know about the local job market. They can point to the employment and certification programs, local leaders in the profession, and the little tricks to getting hired. Many associations maintain placement bureaus or resume files to meet their employment needs, although by law they cannot represent you to employers. They can, however, let you know who is hiring and forward your resume.

Finding these organizations is only sometimes tricky. Often they are listed in the phone book. However, many do not have listings since they are informal or have no permanent addresses or phone numbers. In these cases, you can call someone in the field for information about the local organizations.

Let's say you are an architect or want to work with architects. Look in the yellow pages under "Architects." You see that there is a listing for The American Institute of Architects, Portland Chapter, Inc.: "Offers information on professional services...Qualifications of members — Oregon architectural law...Offers assistance in selecting an architect...." A phone call to this association reveals a "clearing house" with job listings. This enables potential employers to meet with interested and qualified job-hunters. You could have called any architectural firm in Portland and uncovered this association.

By way of examples, I unearthed the following four

organizations and discovered what they offer and how they work:

• 78   **The Portland Advertising Federation [PAF]**
P.O. Box 14067
Portland, Oregon 97214
Executive Secretary: Jack Matlack, 771-4033

The PAF is a local group of advertising professionals who can provide leads, contacts, advice on portfolio preparation, and information about advertising agencies. They maintain a resume file. When a potential employer calls, the PAF screens the resumes and forwards a selected group to the employer. He then does his own interviewing and hiring. The PAF has biweekly luncheon meetings at the Benson Hotel.

The Oregon Chapter of the American
    Marketing Association
P.O. Box 82
Portland, Oregon 97207

Membership in this group consists mostly of junior marketing managers and researchers. The job placement function is called the "Job Mart," where mini-profiles of resumes are included in the monthly newsletter. However, neither the resume file nor monthly meetings are restricted to members. Since there is no phone you must write for a schedule of the meetings.

Public Relations Roundtable
No permanent address or phone

This local organization of public relations people has no national affiliation. The placement service consists of collecting resumes and condensing selected ones for inclusion in the monthly meeting notice. Dick Syring, the on-going membership chairman, is most likely able to answer questions. He maintains his own public relations consulting service. You know where to find him: Yellow Pages, "Public Relations Counselors."

79 •

Public Relations Society of America [PRSA]
Portland Chapter
No permanent address or phone

PRSA is a national association with local chapters. The placement bureau consists of a resume file, and mini-profiles included in the meeting announcements. To locate information about PRSA you might call a local public relations firm.

Other Related Professional Associations:

- Oregon Newspaper Publishers Association
- Oregon Communicators Association
- Women Employed

And there are many, many others — you just have to nose around until you find the ones that can be useful to you.

PRIVATE EMPLOYMENT AGENCIES

• 80

The Better Business Bureau received only three complaints against private employment agencies statewide in 1976, a dramatic decline from the preceding year. That is not to say the industry does not still have PR problems; indeed it does. Rather it is to say that professionals in the field have taken active steps to uplift the reputation of the business; they have been working to improve both their services and their image.

I will keep my promise of giving no endorsements to any agencies or services in this book. However, some notes about employment agencies in general should be useful. Obviously, the agencies can be of service to people. But select the agencies you want to use very carefully. Interview these agencies and counselors. Find out exactly what they can offer to you and how they will do it. Shop around. Be selective. Remember that you are the consumer.

These notes have been condensed from two conversations I had with professionals in the field. One man is the technical placement officer for one of Portland's prominent agencies; the other man owns a successful agency and is the past president of the Oregon Association of Employment Services.

There is a great deal of difference between agencies or counselors which are employer-fee-paid and those which are not. Employer-fee-paid agencies do not require you to sign a contract. You must, however, sign an authorization for them before they can check your references, as you do with applicant-fee-paid agencies. When examining employer versus applicant-fee-paid positions, remember one cold hard fact: The loyalty of an agency or counselor lies with whoever pays the fee. Counselors in employer-fee-paid agencies are working for the companies they serve — they are headhunters. Applicant-paid counselors are working for individuals. However, in some cases they might be eager to place you in almost any position so they can collect their commission.

Applicant-fee-paid agencies can now charge as much as 140% of your first month's salary. In some cases, even if you do not work out in the job, you will still be required to pay the fee. When you go into an agency office you will be asked to fill out a rather long application before you see any counselors. This is when they may ask you to sign the contract. You don't have to sign anything until you have had a chance to interview your counselor and have had the details of the contract and fee schedule explained to you. Know exactly what your liability is before you sign your name to **anything.** Remember that agencies will vary tremendously in the ways they handle financial agreements.

There are some easy ways to find out about a particular agency's reputation. You can call the Oregon State Department of Labor to find out if an agency is licensed and how long it has been licensed. (It is interesting to note that Oregon has some of the stiffest laws regarding employment agencies in the country; licensing, bonding, and operational regulations are very strict.) You might determine whether an agency is nationally affiliated, with job listings nationwide, or whether it is local, preferring to focus on regional placements. Is the agency small, or are there several people on the staff? Some agencies prefer to remain small in order to give more personal service, while others need to be larger to deal more effectively with specialty fields. You might look for personal references from people who have used the agencies.

When checking out agencies, use the telephone! Call to see which ones can meet your needs. This can save you a great deal of time and running around. When interviewing a counselor ask him or her about his own background. There is a move in the more progressive agencies to hire counselors trained in their field of placement, thereby getting away from overly aggressive sales personalities. Above all, know your counselor. Assess his or her listening skills, understanding of your field, and record of success. You should work well together if you like each other.

The Oregon Association of Employment Services (OAES) is the state chapter of the National Employment Association (NEA). Members are sworn to a strict code of ethics covering relations with employers, relations between services, advertising, service charges and collections, and other general matters. For example, the following is excerpted from the NEA's "Standards of Ethical Practices":

"An applicant shall be aware of charges, if any, before being permitted to incur any obligation for services rendered.

"Service will be withheld from employers who are known to abuse or exploit their employees.

"Positions listed in newspapers or other media shall refer to bona fide openings available at the time that copy is given to these publications for insertion."

A copy of these standards is available from the National Employment Association, 200 K Street, N.W. Washington, D.C. 20006.

The highest professional ranking for agency personnel is the Certified Employment Consultant (CEC). This program was established by the National Employment Association to delineate highly trained and experienced professionals. It's similar to a CPA designation in the accounting profession. One must have been in the business two years before he or she is even eligible to take the CEC test. At the time of this writing there are less than 20 CECs in the OAES membership. A job applicant would do well to search them out, however, for you could be confident of their ability and knowledge.

Thirty-five employment agencies are listed in this section. I found them in the phone book and called each one to see what it would indicate as its specialty, and whether it operated as employer-fee-paid (EPF), applicant-fee-paid (APF), or both. That is the extent of the information I present here, along with a note indicating whether the agency is a 1977 member of OAES.

83 •

Abacus
1600 S.W. Fourth, Suite 602
Portland, Oregon 97201
228-3321
Both APF and EPF
Full service

Acme Personnel Service
(five offices, each independently owned)
621 S.W. Morrison
Portland, Oregon 97205
224-5500

Both APF and EPF
Full service

• 84   American Business Consultants
1618 S.W. First
Portland, Oregon 97201
226-3451
EPF
Full service

Beaver Employment Agency
10835 S.W. Canyon Road
Beaverton, Oregon 97005
644-3500
Mostly APF
Full service
OAES member

Brown & Associates, Inc. Agency
610 S.W. Alder
Portland, Oregon 97205
224-6860
Both APF and EPF
Full service
OAES member

Bryant Bureau (Division of Snelling & Snelling)
421 S.W. Sixth, Suite 413
Portland, Oregon 97205
EPF
Executive and Professional
OAES member

CIP Commercial Industrial Personnel Service
522 S.W. Fifth
Portland, Oregon 97204

223-6211
Both APF and EPF
Forest Products, Manufacturing, Utilities and Service
Industries

Career Counseling Center, Inc.
2125 S.W. Fourth
Portland, Oregon 97201
226-3811
Both APF and EPF
Office, Industrial, Technical, Sales
OAES member

CompuSearch (a division of Management Recruiters)
811 S.W. Sixth
Portland, Oregon 97204
224-9575
EPF
Data Processing
OAES member

Career Specialists
404 East 15th Street
Vancouver, Washington 98663
Portland number: 248-9753
EPF
Executive and Sales

Devonshire Personnel of Vancouver, Inc.
1104 Main
Vancouver, Washington 98660
Portland number: 285-2504
Both APF and EPF
Full service

• 86

Dunhill of Portland
806 S.W. Broadway
Portland, Oregon 97205
224-1850
EPF
Full service
OAES member

Executive Resources, Inc.
200 S.W. Market
Portland, Oregon 97201
243-1010
EPF
Executive Search and Placement
OAES member

Employers Exchange — see American Business Consultants

Employment Opportunities, Inc.
510 S.E. Morrison
Portland, Oregon 97214
231-5771
Both APF and EPF
Full service
OAES member

The Executive Suite (a division of Acme)
207 American Bank Building
Portland, Oregon 97205
224-5500
EPF
Executive placement

Field & Associates Professional Personnel & Business
Consultants
7626 N.E. Hazel Dell Avenue
Vancouver, Washington 98665
Portland number: 283-4161
Both APF and EPF
Full service

Hastings Personnel Service
520 S.W. Sixth
Portland, Oregon 97204
228-8518
Both APF and EPF
Full service

Job Exchange
437 S.E. 85th
Portland, Oregon 97216
256-4361
Both APF and EPF
Clerical

The Job Mart — see American Business Consultants

Lake Oswego Employment Agency
342 S.W. "B" Street
Lake Oswego, Oregon 97034
635-4554
Both APF and EPF
Full service; office

The Legal Register — see Wallace & Associates

Management Recruiters of Portland
811 S.W. Sixth
Portland, Oregon 97204
224-8870
EPF
Executive, Sales, Technical, Management
OAES member

Medical Dental and Professional Placement Service, Inc.
628 Medical Arts Building
Portland, Oregon 97205
222-6801
APF
Medical and Dental Professionals

N-R-Getic Help Unlimited
8705 S.E. 17th
Portland, Oregon 97202
233-5876
EPF
Domestic

Northwest Personnel Services (two offices)
506 S.W. Fifth
Portland, Oregon 97204
222-3231
Both APF and EPF
Full service

Office Mates Five (a division of Management Recruiters)
811 S.W. Sixth
Portland, Oregon 97204
224-5540
EPF
All office and clerical
OAES member

Personally Yours
207 E. Tenth
McMinnville, Oregon 97218
472-4142
Full service
OAES member

Professional Search, Inc.
6443 S.W. Beaverton-Hillsdale Hwy.
Portland, Oregon 97221
292-0721
EPF
Engineering and Manufacturing Management

Reese Personnel Inc.
1914 East Burnside
Portland, Oregon 97214
233-5783
EPF
Engineering and Technical

Richards & Richards Personnel Agency
1007 N.E. Broadway
Portland, Oregon 97232
288-8851
Both APF and EPF
Full service
OAES member

Reilly & Associates Personnel Agency
520 S.W. Yamhill, Suite 624
Portland, Oregon 97204
223-2332
Both APF and EPF
Full service
OAES member

• 90

Robert Half Personnel Agencies, Inc.
1 S.W. Columbia
Portland, Oregon 97258
222-9778
EPF
Accounting, Financial, Computer
OAES member

Schedeen Personnel Placement Agency
2324 S.E. 122nd
Portland, Oregon 97233
255-1790
Both APF and EPF
Full service

Snelling & Snelling Agency (six offices)
711 S.W. Alder
Portland, Oregon 97223
243-2424
Both APF and EPF
Full service
OAES member

Tower Personnel Recruiters
5331 S.W. Macadam
Portland, Oregon 97201
222-1651
Both APF and EPF
Full service
OAES member

Vancouver Personnel Service
400 East Evergreen Blvd.
Vancouver, Washington 98660
Portland number: 285-3490
Both APF and EPF
Full service

Wallace & Associates Personnel
610 S.W. Broadway
Portland, Oregon 97205
222-4445
EPF
Legal Personnel

EMPLOYMENT CONTRACTORS

Employment contractors are really temporary employment agencies, but cannot legally be labeled as agencies
since they are not subject to the Oregon State licensing
requirements. All anyone needs to operate as a temporary
help service is a business license.

I think the temporary contractors have a tremendous
value: If you are taking time to do a thorough job of career
planning or to investigate different career options, these
services can be survival sources for you. They can bring in
the money while leaving you free of normal job commitments.

When selecting temporary employment services, you can use the same criteria as you would to select employment agencies and counselors. Remember that you never pay a fee to an employment contractor. Your employer is the employment service itself. Sometimes a temporary position turns into a permanent one; the contractor should have an arrangement with the potential employer in that case and you will not be obligated to engage in any fee arrangements.

The contractors here were, again, obtained from the Yellow Pages of the phone book and investigated with a telephone call. They have different specialties, and you can see from this list which skills are most saleable.

A Temporary Keypunch (also known as N-R-Getic Help)
8705 S.E. 17th
Portland, Oregon 97202
233-5876
A "Girl Friday" service

Accountemps
1 S.W. Columbia
Portland, Oregon 97258
223-8369
Financial and data processing

Barry Services, Inc.
1101 S.W. Alder
Portland, Oregon 97205
243-2444
Clerical, industrial, janitorial

Russell Brown Office Services
314 S.W. Ninth
Portland, Oregon 97205

226-3295
All phases of office work

Dunhill Temps
806 S.W. Broadway
Portland, Oregon 97205
226-0060
Predominantly office; some sales and technical

Employers Overload Company
506 S.W. Sixth
Portland, Oregon 97204
224-3155
Full service

Future Machines Corporation
1815 S.E. Seventh
Portland, Oregon 97214
232-6422
Electronic assembly farm-out labor

Homemakers Upjohn
2125 S.W. Fourth
Portland, Oregon 97201
224-7833
Nursing care

Kelly Services
324 S.W. Stark
Portland, Oregon 97214
227-1711
Office, industrial, marketing, technical

Manpower Temporary Services
535 S.W. Clay
Portland, Oregon 97201

226-3209: Industrial
226-6281: Office, data processing, medical/dental, technical

• 94

Medical Personnel Pool of Portland, Inc.
500 N.E. Multnomah, Suite 337
Portland, Oregon 97232
234-0968
Nursing care

N-R-Getic Help Unlimited (see this listing in agencies)

Professional Drafting, Inc.
1208 S.W. Thirteenth
Portland, Oregon 97205
222-4592
A job shop for drafting needs

Temporarily Yours
1101 S.W. Alder
Portland, Oregon 97205
243-2449
Full service

Western Temporary Services
724 West Burnside
Portland, Oregon 97205
223-6341: Industrial
223-4110: Clerical, marketing, medical

5. Information Sources about Careers, Industries, Companies

A survey of local and national resources available to the serious researcher or the gentle browser.

An effective career-hunting strategy requires information about the occupations and fields which interest you. Successful job interviews depend on your knowing as much about the companies as possible. You also need information about current happenings in the work arena. Even when you are interviewing someone for information about his or her field, you need to have insight into it already so your questions can focus on what you need to learn from that person. Otherwise you waste time asking people about matters that you could find out with five minutes in the library.

There are many useful sources of information about careers, industries, and businesses. The Better Business Bureau has prepared reports on some organizations. The usefulness of professional associations, again, is evident. You can obtain annual reports and house publications from almost all corporations by writing to them or soliciting the local stock brokerages. Of course, never overlook the people you meet. Be nosy. You might discover a connection without any intention of doing so. The Chamber of Commerce in any city will have a wealth of information about specific companies as well as about the area in general. If you are considering relocation, write the Chambers of the cities that interest you to see what kinds of information they will send to you.

The Portland Chamber of Commerce can furnish all kinds of data about the Portland Standard Metropolitan Statistical Area (SMSA). It has assembled a series of publications which you can find at career resource centers in colleges, the public libraries, or the Chamber of Commerce office located at 824 S.W. Fifth in downtown Portland. The publications include:

Portland Metropolitan Manufacturing Firms Employing 26 or More Persons	$3.00
Portland's 100 Largest Employers	$1.00
Real Estate Trends in Portland	$7.50
Economic Base of Portland	$ .25
Distribution Brochure (Summary of Portland's Warehousing and Wholesale Trade Industry)	$ .25
Portland Facts and Living Conditions	$ .25
Colleges of Portland and Oregon	$ .25
Portland's 30 Major Manufacturing Firms	$ .25
Commercial and Industrial Real Estate Firms	free
Business and Vocational Schools	free

Employment Agencies
(includes only Chamber members)   free
Labor Force Trends   free
Current Population and Forecast   free
Some of Oregon's Trade Associations   free
Cost of Living Index   free

There are other publications in the series; a complete list can be obtained from the Chamber office.

Public and college libraries are the greatest resources available to you. They are packed with information, and are not the least bit intimidating if you spend a few minutes poking around to get a feel for where things are. Fortunately, libraries in Portland are not scarce. We have the public library, the Portland State University Library, and a host of private and community colleges with well-staffed libraries open to the public. You're cheating yourself if you don't take advantage of them!

The Multnomah County Public Library is located downtown on S.W. Tenth between Taylor and Yamhill (the 800 block). The Social Sciences and Education rooms are on the second floor with the main card catalog; the Periodical room and microfilm are on the third floor; the Newspaper room is on the lower level. The librarians rotate desks every half hour so that all are acquainted with the entire facility.

These are some of the unique features of the public library:

• A **Local Firms File** is located in the Social Sciences room. If you are investigating a local company, simply find the manila folder under the company name. The folder is stuffed with newspaper clippings about the business.

• The **Annual Reports File** is also in the Social Sciences room. Current stockholders' reports from corporations throughout the United States are filed here; however, reports for local companies are kept in a separate area and you must ask for them at the desk. It seems they disappear when they are filed with the others.

• **Company histories** can be located by using the card catalog on the second floor. Just look under the name of the company.

• **Company publications** (house organs) from local companies are kept in the Periodicals room on the third floor. You can ask a librarian to help you find the ones you need.

• **The Oregonian** and **The Oregon Journal** have been indexed by the library staff. You can locate articles by looking under topic headings. The index is kept in a separate catalog area and you must ask for it at the central information desk on the second floor. The newspapers are on microfilm on the third floor.

• Two little pamphlets you can pick up in the library include **Job Hunting?**, a listing of books that can help with career choice, resumes, resources, testing, and training; and **Northwest Firms,** which lists sources of information about both local and nonlocal companies.

• **Reference materials and trade directories** are shelved in the Social Sciences room. They cover an astonishingly wide range of fields and can be invaluable if you need to locate agencies, firms, and people in an occupational area.

The remainder of this chapter is a bibliography of 62 books, directories, magazines, newspapers, and encyclopedias which can help you in a career or job search. Each one is briefly described so you can see at a glance whether it is a resource you should investigate. I don't pretend to offer a complete list. There are simply too many to compile. Rather, these are some of the widely used sources and overviews which can point you in the direction of further resources.

The bibliography is presented in two parts, with books, directories, periodicals, and indexes enumerated for each.

• 100

Part I includes a list of information sources about careers, schools, specific occupations, and working. Part II presents both general and specific information sources about companies and industries. This takes government, education, health, and social agencies into account as well as labor and corporate concerns. There is a further breakdown between regional and national resources. The libraries generally carry these reference sources, except as noted in the annotation.

A brief description is necessary to explain the number coding systems used in many of these sources. **The Dictionary of Occupational Titles [D.O.T.]** is the Department of Labor's inventory of all jobs in the American economy. This D.O.T. system is universally used to classify jobs; every conceivable occupation has a code number. Also universally applied, the S.I.C. coding system is fully explained in **The Standard Industrial Classifications Manual,** another government endeavor. S.I.C. codes classify industries and businesses—the entire field of economics—by the types of activities in which they are engaged. By using the D.O.T. and S.I.C. systems, great volumes of data can be compared with relative ease. It might seem confusing at first, but this standardized system will make your research much easier.

PART I:
CAREERS, SCHOOLS, OCCUPATIONS, AND WORKING
Local and Northwest Region

Career Information System: Occupational Information, Portland Metropolitan Area (Career Information System, Eugene, Oregon, 1977).

Occupational descriptions are included in this book, providing information about career fields. Job duties, working conditions, aptitudes, employer groups, wages, prospects, and preparation are discussed. The book provides current labor market and educational information on a national and local level. It also lists bibliographical references for additional information about specific occupations.

Careers: A Directory of Vocational and Technical Training Resources in Oregon, 1973 ed. (Graphic Arts Center, Portland, 1972).

This is a cooperative project of the public and private vocational, technical, and counseling resources in Oregon. Designed to provide a systematic approach to selecting a career and occupation, it covers (1) getting to know yourself through personal analysis and inventory, (2) picking the right career by reviewing job descriptions and identifying training needs, (3) choosing the right school by identifying resources, inspecting school facilities, and selecting the school, and (4) getting the job you want by use of effective resumes and interviewing techniques. The manual includes a directory of the vocational training institutions in Oregon.

Directory of Services (State of Oregon Department of Employment, Salem, Oregon, 1971).

All the state services related to employment and labor are compiled in this sourcebook. The nature of each service is supplemented by the address, phone number, and name of the person to contact. The book indicates what resources are available, who they can help, what they do, and how they do it. It is indexed by the name of the agency and the nature of service.

Northwest Education/Employment Directory, 3rd ed. (Jobs Unlimited, Inc., Everett, Washington, 1968).

Although this directory might be outdated, there are useful articles on first jobs, changing careers, resumes, vocational education, financial aid, etc. It includes an occupational outlook of selected occupations in Oregon, Washington, and Alaska. There are also employer listings in business, industry, state and federal governments, and health career fields. These list address, phone, type of business, and the name of the person to contact. Several indexes include apprenticeships and on-the-job training programs.

Oregon Woman's Resource Guide by Marilyn Schmalle-Clark and Nancy Bridgeford (Continuing Education Publications, Portland, Oregon, 1976).

This compilation of statewide resources for women is organized and clearly explained in the following categories: employment, financial information, legal resources, education, children, counseling and personal growth, health and medicine, emergency help, organizations and groups, and communication channels. The text is combined with resource presentation to form a fairly complete guide to meet the needs of women in all areas. The book may be purchased from the Division of Continuing Education on the Portland State University Campus for $3.

National in Scope

American Trade Schools Directory (Croner Publications, Inc., Queens Village, New York, 1957).
103 •
8000 trade, industrial, and vocational schools in the U.S., both public and private, are included in this loose-leaf directory. Section I classifies the schools by trade categories; Section II lists the schools geographically by states and cities. Apprenticeship and vocational training programs are also presented. This is kept up-to-date by monthly supplements.

Career Guide to Professional Associations, 1st ed. (Carroll Press, Cranston, Rhode Island, 1976).
The D.O.T. system is used to arrange professional associations by career classification. Information includes the name of the association, address, comments on educational assistance, employment assistance, standards and ethics, aids, and awards. In Section I, organizations are listed by occupational field. Section II indexes organizations by career field and organization names, while also providing a bibliography.

Career Opportunities. Four separate volumes: **Marketing, Business, and Office Specialists. Engineering Technicians. Agriculture, Forestry, Oceanographic Technicians. Health Technicians.** (J.G. Ferguson Publishing Co., Chicago, Illinois, 1970).
Designed to provide information on a wide variety of job and educational opportunities, these books can help search out careers. The format presents articles about specific career fields with facts about preparation for working in the job, requirements, type of work actually performed, necessary personal qualities, entry-level positions and how to get them, advancement

opportunities, working conditions, earning potential, benefits, and the future of the industry.

• 104

College Placement Annual 1977 (College Placement Council, Inc., Bethlehem, Pennsylvania, 1976).
This yearly manual for graduating college students presents the occupational needs anticipated by 1300 U.S. corporate and governmental employers. Each employer listing explains what the employer does, the kinds of graduates he or she seeks to employ in various fields, and the name of the person to contact. Indexes are occupational and geographical. There are also articles concerning cover letters and resumes, interviewing skills, job changes, first jobs, and career planning.

Encyclopedia of Careers and Vocational Guidance, 3rd ed., 2 vols. (J.G. Ferguson Publishing Company, Chicago, Illinois, 1975).
Information in the directory is compiled to help with individual assessment in relation to occupational opportunities and demands. Articles by national leaders in a variety of industries provide specifics on salaries, educational requirements, advancement possibilities, and other factors. Volume I, **Planning Your Career,** is a general orientation to career fields. It includes ideas about evaluating personal interests, aptitudes, and abilities. Volume II, **Careers and Occupations,** describes 650 occupations with D.O.T. numbers. Articles in this volume concern specific occupations with detailed information about the nature of the work, requirements, employment outlook, social and psychological factors, working conditions, earnings, and sources of additional information.

Dictionary of Occupational Titles, 3rd ed., 2 vols. (U.S. Department of Labor, U.S. Government Printing Office, Washington, D.C., 1965).

The D.O.T. offers the most complete inventory of jobs in the American economy, with an extensive analysis of what each involves and what traits are required of workers. Volume I alphabetizes 21,741 occupations by job titles, with information on what gets done, how it gets done, and why it gets done. Then there are 229 industry designations used with job titles to show where it gets done. Volume II groups jobs having the same basic occupation, industrial, or worker characteristics, implying relationships between occupations.

105 •

Handbook of Job Facts, 4th ed. (Science Research Associates, Inc., Chicago, Illinois, 1968).

As a comprehensive summary of basic trends and features of 300 major occupations, this book can be used as a practical handbook of facts. Each occupation is outlined in terms of duties, main industries where the occupation is found, number of people employed in the occupation, educational and training requirements, advancement and earning potentials, general employment trends, and competition for available jobs. Occupations are arranged alphabetically and indexed by significant title words.

National Directory of Employment Services (Gale Research Company, Detroit, Michigan, 1962).

No newer edition of this directory can be found. Nongovernmental agencies and institutions which can help people find jobs and help employers find employees are compiled here. Information about the agencies include name, address, phone number, chief executive, staffing, founding date, memberships, type of placement or specialties, and other trade names used by the agency. Section I lists private employment agencies, Section II lists educational placement bureaus, and Section III presents employment services offered by business and professional associations.

Occupational Outlook Handbook, 1976-77 (U.S. Department of Labor, U.S. Government Printing Office, Washington, D.C., 1976).

850 occupations and 30 industries are analyzed in terms of job duties, educational requirements, employment outlook, earnings, long-range expectations and fluctuations. This government overview covers the nature of the work, places of employment, training, advancement potential, and sources of further information. There is also attention given to what tomorrow's jobs might be.

Occupational Outlook Quarterly (Bureau of Labor, San Francisco, California).

Quarterly supplemental magazine to **Occupational Outlook Handbook.** Articles concern careers and different aspects of occupations. There is no standard format, but articles of interest appear almost randomly. For example: "Working for Yourself: What's It Like?" "Tailoring: A Trade, A Career," "Foreign Languages and Careers."

PART II:
COMPANIES, INDUSTRIES, AND BUSINESS NEWS
Local and Northwest Region
BOOKS/DIRECTORIES

Contacts Influential, Portland ed. (Influential Contacts Ltd., Portland, Oregon, 1976-77. Revised annually).

This directory indexes all business concerns and key people in the Portland area. Information includes company name, address, phone number, names of key personnel and their titles, S.I.C. code, number of employees, whether the company is headquartered here or a local business or a branch office, and whether the company is a new business. There are five sections: (1) alphabetical by firm name, (2) business by S.I.C. code, (3) business by zip code area, (4) alphabetical listing of names of key executives, and (5) numerical listing by phone numbers. There are editions for several other major metropolitan areas, but they are not available locally.

Directory of Community Services in Clackamas, Multnomah, and Washington Counties (Tri-County Community Council, Portland, Oregon, 1977).

All social agencies in the tri-county area are listed alphabetically and cross-referenced by functional categories. Each entry includes the address and phone number, contact person, description of services, eligibility requirements, area served, and other relevant information. Also prepared by the Community Council, **Where to Turn** is a small pamphlet offering a listing of the health, welfare, and recreation agencies. It is available free of charge from the Community Service Center, 718 West Burnside in downtown Portland.

Directory of Oregon Manufacturers, 1976-77 (State of Oregon Department of Economic Development, Portland, Oregon. Published biannually).

• 108

Very well organized, this directory provides details about 4600 Oregon manufacturers. Section I is an alphabetical listing of all manufacturing firms in the state, with the S.I.C. codes. Section II is a geographical listing of firms by county and city, with the S.I.C. codes and number of employees of each. Section III provides a product listing by S.I.C. codes. Here each manufacturer is portrayed with address, phone, home office, key executives, and importing or exporting activities. Section IV lists all Oregon products alphabetically with the S.I.C. code.

International Trade Directory of Oregon and Southern Washington (Portland Chamber of Commerce, Portland, Oregon, 1973).

As a resource to businesses involved in importing and exporting goods, the directory lists the following information and sources: Import/export firms, commodities imported and exported, consulting engineers in international practice, countries where these firms operate, airlines, railroads, shipping and trucking firms, tug and barge lines, regional ports, banking services, customhouse brokers, freight forwarders, insurance agents and companies, translators, warehousing, and advisory services for international business people.

1976 Portland City Directory (R.L. Polk & Company, Kansas City, Missouri, 1976. Annual publication).

City directories are tremendous sources of information about almost any geographical location in the U.S. They contain essentially the same information: Section I is a classified business directory with the names and addresses of all business concerns in the community. Section II presents an alphabetical list of the names of residents and businesses. Section III is a directory of householders; Section IV is a numerical telephone listing.

Investing in the Great Northwest, by Shannon P. Pratt and Lawrence R. Ross (Willamette Management Associates, Inc., Portland, Oregon, 1975).

The purpose of this book is twofold: to give insight into the workings of investor-owned companies, and to serve as a guide to stocks and bonds from more than 200 Northwest companies. There are topical discussions of the major areas of commercial activity and a comprehensive review of Northwest economics; company discussions are aided by the use of statistics and tables. Companies are ranked by the values of stocks, total assets and revenues, and number of shareholders.

Who's Who in the West 1974-75, 14th ed. (Marquis Who's Who, Chicago, Illinois, 1974).

18,500 names of people in all fields of accomplishment are compiled here from the 13 western states and western Canada. Entries include leading executives and officials in government, business, education, religion, the press, civic affairs, cultural affairs, the arts, law, athletics, science, and pop culture. The alphabetical listing presents each person's position, vital statistics, parents, education, marital status and children, career-related activities, civic activities, political affiliations and activities, military, memberships, awards, religion, business and home addresses, and anything else that can be discovered about the person. There are also **Who's Who** editions for the World, America, the East, the Midwest, etc. Most are kept reasonably up-to-date.

PERIODICALS/INDEXES

Central Classified (Crawford Service Company, Portland, Oregon).
> Published weekly in conjunction with **Nickel Ads.** A newspaper of advertisements only; there is no editorial content in either paper. **Central Classified** accepts private party ads free. There are many help wanted ads; quite a few of them are selected listings placed by the State Employment Service. The ads cover a very wide range, from domestic help wanted to professional. It is not to be overlooked, if a job-hunting method includes checking want ads.

Daily Journal of Commerce (Daily Journal of Commerce, Portland, Oregon).
> Daily business newspaper. This is a detailed account of business in Portland on a day-to-day basis. Topics include construction plans, city notices, utilities, government matters of public record, official calls for bids, Portland building permits, and people in the business news. There are no formal classified ads, but there are help-wanted ads scattered along the bottom of the pages.

The Downtowner (Community Publications, Inc., Portland, Oregon).

Published each Monday. The editorial content of this newspaper is light in nature, spotlighting people, places, and activities of interest to the community. It is packed with ads from a variety of retail outlets and restaurants. There are only a few help-wanted ads in the classified section.

Northwest Investment Review (Willamette Management Associates, Inc., Portland, Oregon).

A biweekly newsletter. As an investment advisor, this newsletter is registered with the Securities and Exchange Commission, and states its purpose as "monitoring the publicly traded securities of the Great Northwest." There are articles about local companies and industries, and regular features about earnings estimates, earnings reports, meeting schedules, and corporate news. It is indexed quarterly by company references.

Northwest Stock Guide (Willamette Management Associates, Portland, Oregon).

Published quarterly. All publicly held companies headquartered or with major operations in Washington, Oregon, Montana, Alaska, Utah, Wyoming, and Hawaii are included in this directory. Companies are indexed by nine industry groups with all financial and market information. One useful regular feature is Reader Service Cards, which the reader can use to receive free annual reports, reprints, and other information.

Oregon Business Barometer (U.S. Bank of Oregon, Portland, Oregon).

Quarterly economic review. A general review, not

specific to companies, this newsletter charts business activity in Oregon, reflecting employment and earnings, housing starts, manufacturing, agriculture, and wood products. As a general overview of employment in the area, it includes a wage and salary index.

• 112

Oregon Business Review (Bureau of Business Research, University of Oregon College of Business, Eugene, Oregon).

Published three times a year. The articles in this periodical tend to concern the more esoteric aspects of business; they are usually general, not particular to companies or even industries. Most of them are written by people affiliated with the University of Oregon College of Business, presenting philosophy about such topics as business education and marketing management.

Oregon Progress Newsletter (State Department of Economic Development, Portland, Oregon).

Published once every two months. This little newsletter is packed with specific articles about business firms and industrial concerns statewide. It is an excellent source, detailing planned expansions and constructions, new contracts, management changes, relocations, regional office development, and much more. Many articles are directly concerned with the interaction between state government and business.

Oregon Times Magazine (New Oregon Publishers, Inc., Portland, Oregon).

Published monthly. A general entertainment magazine; good for getting a feeling for the Portland area. There are some articles directly related to working and jobs, but most concern music, art, eating out, exploring the city, etc. It is packed with advertising, most of it retail.

Portland Magazine (Portland Chamber of Commerce, Portland, Oregon).

Published monthly; available at local newsstands. Covering current local events and people in the news, **Portland** provides a good look at what is going on in art, business, leisure, social services, and state and local government. There is a regular feature entitled "Inside Business" which spotlights local companies, building contracts, earnings announcements, etc. Also this publication is packed with advertisements of local businesses.

113 •

Willamette Week (Independent News, Inc., Portland, Oregon).

Weekly newspaper. The format is that of general news and entertainment with regular articles about current events, music, art, and food. Advertising is local, mostly retail stores and restaurants. A substantial listing of help-wanted ads in the classified section is joined with a column called "Willamette Work," where job-seekers can place ads for jobs.

National in Scope
BOOKS/DIRECTORIES

Directory of American Firms Operating in Foreign Countries, 8th ed. (Simon & Schuster, New York, 1975).

A general discussion of national business activity abroad supplements this listing of 4500 U.S. corporations which control 17,000 foreign enterprises. Section I presents all firms alphabetically with the U.S. address, officers, names of foreign officers, products and services, and countries of operation. Section II lists firms by country of operation.

Dun & Bradstreet Million Dollar Directory 1977, 2 vols. (Dun & Bradstreet Inc., New York, 1976. Revised annually).

• 114   All businesses and individuals with a known net worth of $1,000,000 or more, including industrial concerns, utilities, transportation companies, banks, trust companies, stock brokers, insurance companies, wholesalers, and retailers, are listed in this well-known directory. Volume I presents the businesses alphabetically by name, with the state of incorporation, subsidiaries, address and phone, S.I.C. code, annual sales, and number of employees. Officers, directors, and other principles are named. Volume II includes the businesses geographically and by product classification using 900 S.I.C. codes. Volume II indexes top management by name and position.

Dun & Bradstreet Middle Market Directory 1977.
This directory is just like the **Million Dollar Directory** with two exceptions: It concerns business enterprises in the U.S. which have a known net worth of $500,000 to $999,999, and there is no top-management index.

Encyclopedia of Associations, 11th ed., 3 vols. (Gale Research Company, Detroit, Michigan, 1977).
This valuable resource is a compendium of nonprofit membership organizations, including trade associations, professional societies, labor union, fraternal and patriotic organizations, and other groups with voluntary membership. Each association is listed with address, phone number, founding date, number of members, chief official, staff, number of local groups, description, publications, affiliations, conventions, and meetings. Volume I is organized by topic area. Volume II lists the organization geographically and by the name of the chief executive. Volume III is a

periodical supplement, used to note new associations and projects.

Encyclopedia of Business Information Sources (Gale Research Company, Detroit, Michigan, 1976).
Extremely useful. This directory provides a synthesis of all known fact sources on topics in business, commerce, and industry. It is organized alphabetically by subject category. Sources of information pertaining to that subject are then listed, including encyclopedias, directories, handbooks, manuals, bibliographies,

Directory of U.S. Employers, by K.C. Kraft (Simon & Schuster, New York, 1970).
Information on 1,000 business and industrial firms is presented by Mr. Kraft, whose background is in employment and college recruiting. The book is designed for use by job-hunters and is divided into three categories: Industrial Corporations, Business Firms, and Government/Hospitals/Colleges. Company information includes name, parent firm, address, number of employees, S.I.C. code, financial activity, employment data, recruiting needs, names of officials, and principal divisions. Indexes are alphabetical, geographic, and occupational.

Moody's Analysis of Investments (Moody's Investors Service, Inc., New York, 1977).

A yearly publication with weekly supplements; the analysis is broken into five parts, each treated here as a distinct entity:

Municipal and Government Manual, 2 vols.

This is the most complex of the manuals, covering all governmental agencies and enterprises. Financial statistics and statements are presented. The alphabetical index at the front of the book is extremely helpful in finding federal, state, or local agencies.

Industrial Manual, 2 vols.

An analysis of companies found in the New York Stock Exchange, American Stock Exchange, and regional exchanges. Presents bond and stock descriptions, financial statements, and a long list of details about each company including history, officers, products, number of employees, etc. Information sources are stockholders' reports and the Securities and Exchange Commission. There is also a section with reports on international industrials.

Bank and Finance Manual, 2 vols.

This manual provides all financial information on banks, trust companies, savings and loan associations, federal credit agencies, real estate companies, investment trusts, and insurance and finance companies. Data includes financial statements, stock and bond descriptions, capital structure, history, officers, subsidiaries, and nature of the business. 31,000 banks are analyzed.

Public Utilities Manual, 1 vol.

An analysis of all public utility enterprises (electric, gas, telephone, and water). Information concerns financial statements, capitalization, debts, capital stocks, and all common descriptions of the agencies such as history, officers, rates, franchises, etc.

Transportation Manual, 1 vol.

Includes airlines, steamship companies, railroads, electric railways, auto and truck rental agencies, and all other transportation modes. It provides all financial and background data for public as well as private companies.

Moody's Handbook of Common Stocks, Summer 1977 ed. (Moody's Investors Service, Inc., New York, 1977. Revised quarterly).

944 stocks with high investor interest are presented with basic financial and business information. Moody comments on important characteristics of the company and gives it an assigned investment grade. There are long-term price charts and information about capitalization, interim earnings, dividends, company background, recent developments, prospects, officers, number of stockholders, and annual reports. The companies are presented alphabetically and categorized by industry.

SIE Guide to Business and Investment Books (Select Information Exchange, New York, 1974).

A guide to sources of business and investment information. 8,100 business and investment books in print are analyzed, categorized, and priced. Publications are arranged by subject category.

Standard Industrial Classification Manual (U.S. Government Printing Office, Washington, D.C. 1972).

The S.I.C. system is a universal coding system used to standardize information relating to the entire field of economics. This manual explains the S.I.C. codes. The numbers are ordered with the classification title and a brief description of each.

Standard and Poor's Industry Surveys, 2 vols. (Standard and Poor's Corporation, New York, 1977).

• 118

General comments on the latest developments, market and company statistics, and investment outlooks are presented for 69 major domestic industries. Each is examined in terms of prospects, trends, and problems from both a current and a historical perspective. Leading companies in each industry are compared by growth in sales and earnings; companies are tracked over a ten-year span regarding capital expenditures, profit margins, price-earning ratios, and other data. The text is supplemented with statistical tables and charts.

Standard & Poor's Register of Corporations, Directors, and Executives, 3 vols. (Standard & Poor's Corporation, New York, 1977).

Annual; this is the 50th Anniversary Edition. Volume I lists corporations alphabetically by name. Addresses, names, and titles of officers, accounting firms, S.I.C. codes, annual sales, number of employes, divisions, and subsidiaries are kept current. Volume II lists all directors and executives individually, alphabetically by name. It provides personal data on each, including business affliations, business and home address, places and dates of birth, college and year of graduation, places and memberships. Volume III is a compendium of six indexes, among them a geographic index, a new additions section, and an obituary section.

Standard and Poor's Stock Reports (Standard and Poor's Corporation, New York, 1977. Revised quarterly).

Comprehensive two-page reports are presented for each company whose stock is traded on the New York Stock Exchange, The American Stock Exchange,

regional exchanges, and over-the-counter. These reports are very detailed, with information about the
company's fundamental position, product lines, marketing organization, and research and development
efforts. Complete financial, historical, and market
data is supplemented by Standard & Poor's appraisal
of each company's prospects.

**Thomas Register of American Manufacturers/Thomas
Register Catalog File 1977,** 12 vols. (Thomas Publishing
Company, New York, 1977).

Volumes I through VII group manufacturers under an
alphabetical list of general product categories. Each
company is listed with a tangible assets rating.
Volume VIII presents U.S. manufacturers alphabetically by company name, with address and phone,
names of officers, capital rating, local representatives
and sales offices, asset rating, subsidiaries, and
affiliates. Volumes IX through XII are actual catalogs
used by companies to display their products and
services.

U.S. Industrial Outlook 1977 (U.S. Department of Commerce, Washington, D.C., 1977).

• 120

Highlights of various industry sectors are presented with a statistical capsule of each, covering size in terms of shipments, employment, number of establishments, competitive trade position, and growth history. The Wholesale Price Index shows the extent of price changes since 1967. The narrative portrays the current developments and influential factors affecting each industry. Trends, projections, and long-range forecasts complete the report.

Walker's Manual of Western Corporations, 68th ed., 2 vols. (Walker's Manual, Inc., Long Beach, California, 1976).

Detailed reports of companies headquartered in the 13 western states and western Canada include the following information: Name, address, description of business, acquisitions, number of shareholders and employees, capitalization, officers and directors, cash dividends and other market information, balance sheets, debentures, debts, auditors, legal counsel, transfer agents, incorporation date, meeting dates, and litigations or other pertinent information. Reports are indexed alphabetically, by geographic area, and by industry classification.

PERIODICALS/INDEXES

'76 Ayer Directory of Publications (Ayer Press, Philadelphia, Pennsylvania, 1976).

Publications are arranged by geographic location, with information regarding advertising rates, subscription prices, circulation, frequency of publication, basic editorial content, editors' names, and other relevant data. No internal publications are included. The directory is indexed by 900 subject classifications.

Business Periodicals Index (H.W. Wilson Company, Bronx, New York, 1977).
Published monthly with yearly bound cumulations. Approximately 165 business periodicals are indexed. Subject entries are alphabetical; articles about companies are found under the name of the company. Author listings at the back of the book refer to book reviews. The subject entry "Growth Firms" is especially helpful because it lists firms which are expanding and may be receptive to an enterprising jobhunter.

Christian Science Monitor, Western edition (Christian Science Publishing Society, Boston, Massachusetts).
Daily newspaper. Intended to be national and international in scope, this news magazine presents articles covering most national events. Articles often relate to the nation's employment problems and the government's efforts to solve them. The classified ads present some nationwide employment opportunities.

Fortune (Time, Inc., Chicago, Illinois).
Widely read monthly business magazine. This magazine is famous for publishing the **Fortune 500** yearly, generally in May. The top 500 industrials in the U.S. are ranked according to sales, assets, net income, stockholder's equity, number of employees, earnings per share, and revenue to investors. There is also a group profile of the 500, and an analysis of who did the best and worst among them.

Funk and Scott Index of Corporations and Industries (Predicasts, Cleveland, Ohio).

Weekly and monthly, with yearly cumulations. 750 financial publications, business newspapers, trade magazines, and special reports are indexed. Subject material includes corporate acquisitions and mergers, new products, technological developments, trends in business and finance, and corporate management and labor relations. There is a brief description of article content.

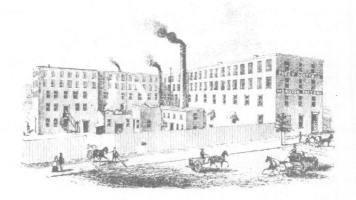

Gebbie House Magazine Directory, 9th ed. (National Research Bureau, Burlington, Iowa, 1976).

Gebbie is self-described as "a public relations and freelance guide to the nation's leading house magazines." The internal and external house organs of more than 3,000 companies, clubs, and governmental agencies are listed with information about the sponsor of the publication, editor's name, frequency of issue, size, circulation, and editorial policy. There is a geographical listing and a breakdown of industries. These could be invaluable in investigating companies of interest of job-hunters.

The Kiplinger Washington Letter (Kiplinger Washington Editors, Washington, D.C., 1977).

A weekly newsletter, cleverly written. Offers concise general information on national business trends and effects of government activity. It covers all kinds of issues with predictions about the economy, government, people, court decisions, etc.

123 •

The Standard Periodical Directory, 5th ed. (Oxbridge Communications, Inc., New York, 1977).

The 60,000 U.S. and Canadian publications listed in this directory include consumer magazines, trade journals, newsletters, and government publications. Each entry lists the publisher's name and address, names of editors, description of content, year established, subscription rate, circulation, and additional information. They are arranged alphabetically by classification, and are cross-referenced by key words. The index presents a list of all entries by publication title.

The Value Line Investment Survey (Arnold Bernhard & Company, Inc., New York).

Published weekly in 3 sections. Sections I and II rank 88 industry groups according to probable market performance over the next 12 months. The analyses of industries are extremely current with a yearly outlook and predictions for the next year. These are followed by analyses of companies within each industry. Section III is kept in a separate volume. It is a weekly newsletter spotlighting selected companies, industries, and investment strategies.

Wall Street Journal (Dow Jones and Company, Inc., 1977. Western edition published daily in Palo Alto, California).

A widely read and respected business daily newspap-

• 124

er, the **Journal** is an excellent way to keep in touch with the entire economic picture of the U.S. Regular features include "What's News" and "Who's Who." The latter spotlights new management—people who might need fresh blood in their organization. "The Mart" is the classified section. The Western edition carries ads for business executives in all fields, but many of these are blind ads. The best days to find ads for available positions are Tuesdays and Wednesdays.

The Wall Street Journal Index (Dow Jones Books, Princeton, New Jersey, 1977).

Annual; some libraries carry monthly indexes as well. Obviously, this is a guide to **The Wall Street Journal.** Section I concerns corporate news; the articles are found under the names of the companies. Section II covers general news and is alphabetized by subject headings. There are brief descriptions of the article content. Dow Jones averages for the year can be found in the back of the book.

Wall Street Transcript (Wall Street Transcript Corporation, New York).

Published each Monday; cost is $15 for single issue. Self-described as "the Information Center for Business and Finance," this newspaper offers company studies, industry surveys, corporate reports, market analyses, financial statements, and business news in all forms. Articles are quite detailed. Regular features include "Who's Who in Profits" and "The Executive's Corner."

6. Career Pitfalls You Can Avoid

A case-by-case discussion of job-hopping, poor skill evaluation, dead-ending, reentry problems, and lack of career direction. A look at possible solutions and a few individuals who have successfully redirected themselves.

Sometimes the problems of selecting or implementing career goals are totally intimidating. You feel as though you can't move. There are so many choices, so many directions, so many other people trying to take **your** job. Sometimes you wish you were six years old again.

And yet the work must be done, for your career is critically important to your total life and well-being. The process of setting goals, personal and professional, is imperative if you are to be in control of what happens to you rather than controlled by what happens to you. And once is not enough! Goal-setting is constant. You find that you have to review these goals periodically to assure that they are still consistent with your other life values. Your work is never done. But you will find that this process becomes exciting as you reap the rewards. You are, after all, concerning yourself with **you.**

Yet the initial process can be intimidating. The inability to change career directions can be due to many things: fear, confusion, social pressure, lack of direction, or practical limitations such as age, education, money, geographic location, and other commitments. You might find that you are locked into a career or way of life which is very difficult to change.

This chapter describes some of the common barriers to career change. You meet some people who have encountered these problems and have attempted to solve them. Some have been successful; others have not.

The Job-Hopper

The problem comes from both directions: the company and the employee. As you might expect, this pattern can be found in low-level, clerical, or entry-level positions. Some industries, too, are plagued with job-hopping, such as restaurants and telephone sales. From the employee's side, there is a general lack of direction. He or she needs a job, and this one is available. Little planning or consideration is given to whether the job fits with other plans. From the company's side, management rarely asks the employee about his or her goals and whether they may be recognized within the company.

SOLUTION

- A continual update of personal and career goals.

- A company program of defining advancement opportunities within the company for new employees.

Case: Gayle is secretary to the vice-president of a Portland-based insurance company. It is her fourth job this year. Before this she was a cashier at a restaurant, a bartender at several eating establishments, and a receptionist at an investment company; she has been at her present job for five months. In previous years she worked as a fitting model, inventory clerk, bartending instructor, and waitress.

Gayle is a smart young woman with a great deal of energy; she has simply had a hard time harnessing it into an occupation where she could feel fulfilled. Her education consists of two years of general studies at three colleges; she has not been working toward a degree.

Recently I saw her. She had been feeling restless and unhappy with herself, but is now involved with the State Employment Service in a vocational testing program. She has also enrolled in three courses at a local community college. Subject: Business Law. She has had an interest in law for several years, but does not feel that law school is suited to her. She is enthusiastic about her new interests. Combined with vocational counseling, the courses she is taking may direct her to a concrete goal such as a paralegal or legal secretary.

Gayle likes her present job well enough, but knows it does not afford her much mobility. In this light, she will probably not stay there.

However, she hopes the next move will be a careful one, reflecting her new goals and training. She knows that her job-hopper image makes her appear as an employment risk, and so she is staying with her present company until she feels confident of her next move. This, she feels, will be a positive step rather than an impulsive hop.

The Skilled Person with No Skills or Experience

You find this individual sulking in a meaningless job with no avenues for advancement. He or she tells you that he possesses no skills of value—that he never had the opportunity to earn an education, or never had the breaks to get into a "good job."

In reality, these people have an abundance of untapped potential. But they often feel they have been slighted by one or more elements in "the system" and will never be good enough to have a job where they can amount to anything. Maybe they can type a little, but certainly not well enough to get a job as a secretary. Or perhaps they can get along well with people, but could never have a job where they had to tell others what to do. In short, these people tend to underestimate themselves and their potential for successful careers.

SOLUTION

- Vocational aptitude counseling (which shows that everyone can do **something**).

- Vocational training programs to develop basic skills for employment.

Case: My friend Carol is one of the most attractive young women in the city. She turns heads wherever she goes. She used to think her appearance was vital to her existence — that if she looked anything less than spectacular no one would consider her opinions or attest to her value as a human being.

I met Carol when she was working on temporary assignment as part of an eight-member secretarial pool. Her office skills were as good as those of the other members, and her appearance and personality were far superior. Yet she did not indicate her willingness to take on the responsibilities of managing the office when it was clear that she was considered for the job. When the assignment ended a year and a half later, she was in the same position as when she started.

She decided against looking for another job right away. Apathy set in; she found that she did not care much what she did. After four months of clothes shopping, tennis lessons, and cooking for her husband (who had, incidentally, begun to think Carol was becoming a bit dull), Carol realized that she was just not happy. She, too, suspected that she was becoming a bit dull.

She enrolled in a local business college. It did not take her long to realize that her office management skills were already quite polished. She was at the head of her class! She had not known that she had such high skills. With this bit of confidence, she began to work strenuously at developing a high degree of skill in shorthand and typing.

She is almost finished with school, and has a part-time job (to become full-time in the near future) with the local office of a prominent national firm. She has an eye to administrative positions, and now knows that she can perform them as well as anyone.

Carol is certain of her abilities and direction. She has included a personal statement on her resume which reads:

I am an energetic young woman currently enrolled in a local business college to refine my office management and clerical skills. I am eager to work with a progressive well-established company where I can combine my business experience with my office talents. I am serious about my career. My long-term goals include a responsible position with potential for personal and professional growth.

She has come a long way from the woman who would not volunteer to take a higher level job. And she is certainly not dull.

The Middle-Age Career Switcher

Women returning to the job market after years at home: it's becoming a familiar sight. They bring carefully earned degrees and valuable experience into their job interviews. They are usually quite serious about both their education and their careers, a testament to their maturity.

Another familiar story: middle-aged men who have caught themselves midway on the road to workaholism and redirected their career energies. Typically, they are former executives who elected to restrict themselves to less than 50 work hours a week, spend time with their families in leisure activities, and integrate all areas of their lives.

Many of these mid-life career changers are successful in their new pursuits. But many of them suffer from delusions about their employability. They think that age discrimination doesn't exist, just because it is against the law; they take degrees in fields which are limited; they fall victim to career counselors who offer them false hopes and relieve them of their money.

SOLUTION

• Careful research into fields to determine feasibility of fulfilling careers.

• An awareness about career counselors who will take advantage of a client's lack of information.

Case: Mary is 48, blond, svelte, and vivacious. I understand from her friends that this is a transformation, but it is hard to imagine her any other way. She works in a vocational guidance agency helping women return to the work world. Her credibility is indisputable; she is one of the many working women who raised a family and engineered a husband through the critical stages of his early career before deciding on a career for herself.

She is not bitter in any way. She is, in fact, happy with her marriage and pleased with the progress of her children. She is also fortunate that her family is supportive of her extradomestic role. She had been married for 24 years before she focused on her own career interest: the field of vocational counseling. It meant additional education. A bright woman, she had no trouble obtaining the degrees she needed. She was hired by a nonprofit progressive social agency where she uses her skills to help other people like herself.

Case: Leah is almost 50. She, too, raised a family and cared for a husband through his years of graduate school and early professional duties. She was, like Mary, the dutiful wife who provided the social environment her husband needed to succeed in his field. He became quite well known in scholarly circles for his innovative contributions to psychotherapy.

While Leah provided a base of support for him, she did not keep pace with his academic interests. As so often happens, he decided that he had outgrown his wife. He left her.

She began to career-hunt with fervor. She talked with several vocational counselors and explored career alternatives, to no avail. She had been out of the work world too long and had unrealistic expectations of her potential for career success. She received little encouragement from her friends or family.

Leah is bitter. She feels that she was left behind— tricked into a lifestyle that afforded her no growth. She feels that the expectations of women returning to work in mid-life are overly optimistic, "The attitudes that we are old and used up do prevail. No law can change what people think."

Case: Charles' resume looks like an obituary. How could anyone have done all that in one lifetime? Ambition!

At 54, Charles has found that he is not happy in the corporate structure. He wants to spend time with his son, who is almost grown. He has had enough of 60-hour work weeks and lost weekends. He is tired of the corporate pressures which, he thinks, produced his ulcer.

He resigned from his job as administrative vice-president of a local sales company to work with clients on a part-time consulting basis. He is now self-employed and enjoys the freedom to pick and choose his clients. He feels that he can help young businesses avoid some of the common pitfalls.

He admits that this occupation entails a significant

decrease in his income, but he has decided that his personal well-being outweighs the loss of money.

The Corporate Executive Over the Hill at 45

It's easy to recognize this individual. He* is the one at the end of the bar, dreading the thought of going home, dreading the thought of going back to work.

In his 20's, this person is hired into a corporation on a low management level. Showing enthusiasm and promise, he catches the attention of his superiors and begins his long climb to success. He marries, begins a family, and works for the company. During his climb to the top he forgets to remember that he is a human being with a life outside the company. He begins to spend less and less time with his family and more and more time at his job. It eventually becomes all-consuming.

And then one day he hits a dead end. He is approximately 45. He is at the top of his specialty. He cannot make more money. He cannot advance within the company. He is too old to start over in a new industry; besides, he could never get to his present level without years of work. He turns around and finds that his kids have grown up without him. His wife is someone he doesn't know. Oh yes, she knows him: The Money Machine. The company knows him, too: The Company Machine. The Worker.

I realize this bleak picture is an exaggeration in most cases. But it reflects a serious problem: Many successful corporate executives never stop during their climb to the

---

*This pattern is typically exclusive to male executives for two reasons: (1) Just about all executives are men, and (2) the women who make it into upper management are usually extraordinary in the first place and are less likely to suffer common syndromes.

top to assess their career goals in relation to their personal goals. They share a lack of awareness about what is important to them. The result is often disastrous: job

• 134   termination, alcoholism, divorce, and even suicide in extreme cases.

SOLUTION

• The company and the executive must have a mutual periodic updating of career goals. This is the only way the company can ensure that it will benefit from the experience and dedication of the executive. It is also the only way the executive can contribute his total energy to his job while he is there, yet still be in touch with his personal values.

Case: John is sitting in southern California—unemployed, divorced, and so low on money that he has been forced to sell his Porsche. Last year at this time he was maintaining two apartments in two states, commuting between his home in California and his job in Portland, and earning $6,000 a month in a management consulting job. He is 38 years old.

John's professional experience is impressive. He worked for four major American corporations and, most recently, for one of the country's leading financial analysts. He was the star student in his Master's program in Industrial Engineering. The school sent him around the country to shop for a computer system for the college. He is considered in business circles to be an expert in management analysis and administration. In short, he is an accomplished professional with many skills to offer a prospective employer.

He is also what I would call an executive alcoholic. He was working 80 hours a week in Portland and sleeping 45; the remainder of his time was spent mostly in bars and restaurants. Drinking was easy, accessible, and dulled the tension of the days.

His wife in California began to demand that he spend more time at home. (He made it there about once every three weeks.) Their relationship, which had weakened through the years, broke down beyond repair. His two young sons were practically strangers.

In the meantime, his Portland job was becoming excessively demanding. He would be called to meetings on the spur of the moment in the late evenings and on weekends. He was expected to cancel any plans immediately if his boss wanted to use him. He was given increasing administrative responsibilities. The more he worked, the more his boss demanded of him. Other employees began to channel their frustrations and complaints through him. His morale deteriorated. He reached a point where he actually began to behave like a machine— speaking in monotones, walking stiffly, staring blankly at people. He had been sucked of his energy. He was fired.

After a few weeks of stunned inactivity, he decided to reexamine his career goals. He worked with a vocational counselor who helped him delineate areas where he could use his talents. He liked environmental issues, so he tried to research the role his skills could play in that area. He found almost nothing. His career reevaluations did not afford him any specific new directions.

Although he is back to looking for work in his previous field, he has the advantage of having examined his personal values. He feels sure that he will not fall victim to corporate pressures again—if he can find a job, that is. It seems that the $50,000-a-year jobs are quite scarce. Not only are they hard to find, but they are usually grabbed by people who are already employed. There is a great deal of executive stealing at this level of management.

At the time of this writing, John's story does not have a happy ending. He finds it hard to job-hunt in the face of the gloomy prospects, and he frequently wrestles with bouts of depression. But his determination, combined with his professional talents, are his strengths. And next time he will be certain that his chosen paths do not end up in dead ends.

Overeducated, Underemployed, with Delusions of Success

The problem originates with the educators and perpetrators of the myth that good grades and lofty degrees insure career success. It is completed by apathy on the part of students. People who fall victim to these myths are generally bright little kids favored by parents and teachers. They breeze through a liberal arts education, both undergraduate and graduate, contributing significantly to stimulating discussions and the development of theory. However, they find themselves at the end of their academic careers with little more than unrealistic expectations of job opportunities and exaggerated confidences.

The serious problems of underemployment result from student laziness combined with a kind of education hoax. We have all heard stories about the fellow with a Ph.D. in Sociology who earns his living by flipping burgers at the corner fast-food stand. Too often we are tricked into pursuing an educational goal without knowing where and how that knowledge can be used to bring in money—real money for real food in the real world.

SOLUTION

- Educational institutions which require students to continually examine their college programs in terms of actual career goals.

- Vocational guidance throughout grade school, high school, and college to offer students ways to explore occupational fields as well as alternatives to college educations.

- Students who assess their work values in light of realistic environments and employment outlooks.

Case: A young woman, recently employed as a college instructor, is a 1974 graduate with a Master of Science degree in Communication Research. If you ask her what is meant by Communication Research, she begins talking to you in academeze: "Well, it's the study of interactional patterns among individuals or groups, including institutions, as well as message appeals which reflect particular audience analyses...." Blah, blah, blah.

Graduate school was, like undergraduate school, an extension of the protective arm of society. She did not have to get out in that dirty world and beg for a job. She could remain nestled in the arms of academia, letting it stroke her with high grades and the scholarly interest of professors.

There was one time she had to meet with a "degree committee" to approve her graduate program. She told them she wanted to "work in business communications, where I can consult and solve employee and interpersonal group problems.'' OK, they said. The suspicion never crossed her mind that, maybe, one did not come out of graduate school at the age of 24 and expect to be hired as a consultant by major corporations. She suspects, now, that her program advisers thought she might get married and not have to worry about a **real** career — so they let her enjoy her last fling at school. She did not get married. She wanted to go to work.

After four months of looking, she found a job in Portland as communications officer for a small direct selling firm. The company folded six months later, leaving her without even a claim to unemployment compensation.

She resumed looking for a job in advertising, market research, communication consulting, training, development, writing, editing, etc. She walked into ad agencies and said she could do anything (almost). They thanked her for coming and said they would file her resume with the others (approximately 400) and call her when they had an opening in her area.

For the next 18 months she worked as a waitress, bartender, freelance copywriter, interviewer, and waitress. Her resume reshaped itself several times. Eventually, she became depressed. She felt worthless. She could not even type! How did she ever expect to amount to anything?

Finally a friend gave her a copy of ''What Color Is Your Parachute?'' which she read warily. Eureka! She learned she was normal — that many people were in her boat, that underemployment as a result of sloppy educational goals was a common problem which could be solved in ways other than suicide!

She followed with vocational counseling and testing. Business management? An MBA would take two years and much money. So she began to interview people about their own jobs, taking the approach that she would choose her own employer. Her interviews were successful; she even got job offers! However, she made a conscious choice to postpone taking a job for just a bit longer.

She had learned a great deal about career exploration. She had discovered a wealth of resources to help with vocational problems. But most importantly, she had a firsthand knowledge of the hell a person can experience in looking for work unsuccessfully. She wanted to do something about it.

As you have undoubtedly figured out by now, this book is it.

FEEDBACK

Please! Let me know your reactions!

- Did I forget something important?
- Have you discovered any information to be out-of-date?
- Is the information helpful to you?
- What suggestions do you have for improvements?

I would like to hear from you, and will respond personally if I can. A book like this can always be better, if I know your needs and expectations.

Write to me: Sheri Raders
                 P.O. Box 402
                 Portland, Oregon 97207

INDEX